SUCCESSFUL ENTREPRENEURSHIP

Successful Entrepreneurship

Confronting Economic Theory with Empirical Practice

C. Mirjam van Praag

Associate Professor of the Economics of Organization, Department of Economics, University of Amsterdam, The Netherlands

Edward Elgar
Cheltenham, UK • Northampton, MA, USA

Published by
Edward Elgar Publishing Limited
Glensanda House
Montpellier Parade
Cheltenham
Glos GL50 1UA
UK

Edward Elgar Publishing, Inc.
136 West Street
Suite 202
Northampton
Massachusetts 01060
USA

A catalogue record for this book
is available from the British Library

ISBN 1 84376 161 0

Printed and bound in Great Britain by MPG Books Ltd, Bodmin, Cornwall

Contents

Figures

Tables

Acknowledgements

I first planned this book together with Edward Elgar in the fall of 2000. In the meantime, I did some new work, besides writing this book. Therefore, the book is now an extended and altered (I hope improved) version of the original plan.

Chapters 2, 3, 5, and 6 have been based on my PhD thesis. I want to express my gratitude to the supervisors of this thesis, Mars Cramer as well as Joop Hartog. They have been (and still are) of great help and inspiration for my work.

Moreover, chapters 2, 3, 4, 5, and 6 are based on journal publications. Chapter 2 is based, in part, on a publication in *De Economist* in 1999 (van Praag, 1999), Chapter 3 in *Kyklos* in 1995 (van Praag and Van Ophem, 1995), Chapter 4 in *The Journal of Economic Behavior and Organization* in 2002 (Cramer et al., 2002), Chapter 5 on a publication in *Economica* in 2001 (van Praag and Cramer, 2001), and Chapter 6 on a publication in *Small Business Economics* in 2003 (van Praag, 2003).

Last but certainly not least, I am very grateful to the co-authors involved in these journal publications, as well as those co-authors involved in the preparation of future journal publications on which chapters 7 and 8 of this book have been based. Chapter 3 is a spin-off from work with Hans van Ophem, Chapter 4 with Mars Cramer, Joop Hartog and Nicole Jonker, and Chapter 5 with Mars Cramer. Chapter 7 is based on joint works with Justin van der Sluis, Wim Vijverberg and Arjen Van Witteloostuijn (van der Sluis, van Praag and Vijverberg, 2003; van der Sluis, van Praag and Van Witteloostuijn, 2004). Chapter 8 is based on joint work with Niels Bosma and Gerrit De Wit (van Praag, Bosma and De Wit, 2003). Finally, parts of chapters 7 and 8 have been reviewed in an overview article by van der Sluis and myself (van der Sluis and van Praag, 2004). Thanks to the great topic that the economics of entrepreneurship is and to the stimulating environment that these people, amongst other colleagues, have created I greatly enjoyed working on all of the chapters of this book. I hope you enjoy reading them.

C. Mirjam van Praag
Amsterdam, January 2005

PART I

INTRODUCTION

1 Introduction: successful entrepreneurship

That the existence of a problem of knowledge depends on the future being different from the past, while the possibility of the solution of the problem depends on the future being like the past. (Knight [1921] 1971, p. 311)

Relevance
In this book I confront economic theory about entrepreneurship with the determinants of successful entrepreneurship that I find in empirical practice. Before presenting the results of my investigation of these determinants, the relevance and importance of the subject of entrepreneurship in general, and the determinants of successful entrepreneurship in particular are discussed.

Today, most economists and other practitioners of behavioural sciences as well as politicians will readily admit the importance of the entrepreneur's role in society. Entrepreneurs are held responsible for economic development, by introducing and implementing innovative ideas. These ideas include product innovation, process innovation, market innovation and organizational innovations. The (successful) implementation, initiated by entrepreneurs, of these new ideas gives rise to the satisfaction of (new) consumer wants and to the creation of firms. The created firms engender economic growth and supply jobs for the working population. Hence, by stimulating both a product and a labour market, entrepreneurs can be given credit for a considerable contribution to the economy. These are the benefits pertaining to successful entrepreneurship.

Unfortunately, not all entrepreneurs are successful. Too many of them fail: they do not arrive at the stage of employing personnel; they are not in a position to turn their business into a sufficiently profitable organization; their ventures fail to survive the first period at all; or even worse, they go bankrupt. These are the private, psychological and most importantly, social costs pertaining to unsuccessful entrepreneurship.

Instruments are needed to obtain fiscal, social, informational and/or educational policy measures to improve efficiency in the market for entrepreneurs. Market efficiency is improved whenever the number of successful start-ups increases and/or the number of unsuccessful start-ups decreases.

Determinants of entrepreneurial start-up and performance can serve as these instruments. By combining these determinants, one gains insight into current inefficiencies. By means of these instruments, potentially unsuccessful start-ups can be prevented or, even better, turned (in time) into

3

successful ones. Moreover, potentially successful entrepreneurs who do not start because they have neither the willingness nor the opportunity to do so, can be motivated and/or offered this opportunity.

The instruments could find application not only among governmental policymakers. Bankers and other capital lenders could also use them for their own and the entrepreneur's benefit.

Objective

The objective of this book is to answer the following research questions:

- Which factors contribute to the explanation of the observation that some individuals have the opportunity and willingness to become an entrepreneur and others do not?
- Which factors contribute to the explanation of the performance of entrepreneurs? What is the measured impact of the most important factors influencing venture performance?

The answers to these questions imply an answer to the underlying composite question: 'What are the determinants of successful entrepreneurship?'. The empirical analyses underlying the answers to these questions are rooted in (historical) economic theory. They pertain to a sample of young male US citizens and to various samples of Dutch individuals.

The potential determinants of successful entrepreneurship are derived from theory and existing empirical evidence. They include human capital variables, financial variables, risk attitude, psychological variables, macroeconomic variables and (parental) background variables.

Positioning

Knowing that other behavioural disciplines, such as social psychology, are also concerned with entrepreneurship, it would be naive not to acknowledge their fruitful scientific results in the analysis. I shall include some of the common results, but at the same time, I do not want to be guilty of conceit or imply that I, as an economist, am in a position to address the psychological approaches to entrepreneurship competently. Therefore, this book can be positioned as an economic one within the field of social sciences.

Within the field of economics research, this book can be positioned as microeconomic as opposed to macroeconomic. The central unit is the individual entrepreneur, who is likened to other entrepreneurs. I do not compare the proportion of entrepreneurs in a specific country and year to the proportion in other countries and/or years. However, indicators of the macroeconomic environment are included as explanatory factors for individual behaviour.

Within the field of microeconomics, the approach is labour market rather than business oriented: the focus is on the entrepreneur's occupational choice and success, rather than on the enterprise. None the less, enterprise-related variables are included in the research as factors that potentially affect entrepreneurial performance.

A definition of successful entrepreneurship

Definitions of an entrepreneur

Within the course of the empirical work in this book, the following definitions of an *entrepreneur* are used:

- An entrepreneur is someone who indicates either that (s)he has started a business venture alone or with a group or that (s)he has acquired a (family) business, alone or with a group.
- An entrepreneur is someone who acknowledges that s(he) is being the sole owner of a corporation or is self-employed. Self-employed people do not derive their main income from a wage or a salary, but by exercising their profession or business on their own account and at their own risk.[1]

The selection of these two definitions is motivated by their availability in samples that allow empirical analyses in general and by their availability in the Dutch and American samples used for this study in particular. Moreover, these definitions allow a comparison with other empirical person-oriented studies of entrepreneurship. Empirical definitions of entrepreneurship are, in general, fairly comparable, though their meanings are much more prosaic than those in most (untestable) theories that refer to the innovative free mind of the resourceful spiritual entrepreneur. Indeed, most researchers empirically define entrepreneurs as self-employed (van der Sluis et al., 2003).

It is readily admitted that these (as well as other) definitions of an entrepreneur are not perfect. In reality, the difference between an entrepreneur and a non-entrepreneur is not clear. There is rather a continuum of labour market positions stretching from 'totally non-entrepreneurial' to 'heavily entrepreneurial'. Therefore, it is difficult to define a cut-off point on this continuum such that an individual is considered an entrepreneur on one side of the point and not on the other. The concept itself is not defined so uniformly and one-dimensionally.

By utilizing the above definitions, the problem of a researcher having to decide whether an individual's labour market position is sufficiently

entrepreneurial and labelling him or her as an 'entrepreneur' is circumvented. Respondents themselves indicate whether they are entrepreneurs.
In this respect, the definitions are subjective ones. The possibility is
acknowledged that of two individuals, who have identical labour market
positions, one becomes an entrepreneur and the other does not.

There are many more rather theoretical definitions of an entrepreneur
which will be reviewed in due course (see Chapter 2). Finally, in order to
simplify the reading of this book, entrepreneurs are always referred to as
males. At present as well as in the past, most entrepreneurs have been male.

Definitions of success
There is little alignment among researchers on the appropriate performance measure of success in entrepreneurship. At least ten different measures are used. From a recent meta-analysis (van der Sluis et al., 2003) it was
deduced that 47 per cent of studies analysing performance focus on self-
employment earnings – annual, monthly or hourly – which is then entered
in linear or logarithmic form.[2] Another 16 per cent look at inputs (typically
employment or personnel) as a measure of size or growth. Fifteen per cent
examine exit or survival, which can easily be calculated from each
other. Fourteen per cent of studies found other performance measures to
analyse, such as self-employment income as a share of total household
income, a private benefit–cost ratio, the growth rate of profits, a business
diversification index and so forth. In this book, I shall analyse common
performance measures that are used in the literature.

The *indicators of success* or *performance measures* that are utilized in
Parts III and IV are as follows:

- The more personnel an entrepreneur has under his control, the more
  successful he is. This definition is utilized in Chapter 5.
- The longer an entrepreneur survives as such, the more successful he
  is. This definition is used in Chapter 8. More specifically, the longer
  an entrepreneur survives before exiting the entrepreneurial state
  involuntarily, the more successful he is.[3] This definition is utilized in
  Chapter 6.
- The higher the profit of the entrepreneur's firm, the more successful
  the entrepreneur is. This definition is utilized in Chapter 8.
- The higher self-employment earnings are, the more successful the
  entrepreneur is. This definition is used in Chapter 7.

Outline of the book
There are few issues in labour market economics that have already been the
subject of so much research for such a long time as is the case with the

current research subject. Chapter 2 reviews some important contributions to the historical knowledge base of the theory of entrepreneurship. No attempt has been made to survey this knowledge base completely. The idea is to answer some research questions related to the subject of the book in order to provide the reader with an understanding of the development of the theory of (successful) entrepreneurship. The seminal contributions selected are reviewed chronologically and then compared. Finally, an overview is given of the components of the diverging contributions that are empirically testable. The tests themselves are performed and commented on in the empirical chapters that follow in Parts II–IV.

Part II discusses empirical studies of entrepreneurship selection, or venture creation, whereas Parts III and IV discuss factors affecting entrepreneurial success, or venture performance.

Chapter 3 (Part II) develops an empirical model within a dynamic framework to find the determinants of the decision of labour force participants to start up as an entrepreneur. The model separates 'opportunity' and 'willingness' as unobserved factors in the decision to start. In contrast with recent contributions, the distinction between entrepreneurial opportunity and willingness is quite prominent in the classical literature (see Chapter 2).

It is reasoned that only those labour force participants start up as entrepreneurs who are both willing and have enough opportunity to do so. If either or both of these concepts do not exceed their respective threshold values, an individual is observed to remain a non-entrepreneur.

The estimation results of the model that identifies opportunity and willingness based on partial observability of either construct pertain to young white male Americans. They suggest that the majority of young Americans are willing to switch to entrepreneurship but that opportunity is a major constraint, especially through finance. Entrepreneurial ability aspects that can compensate for a lack of capital are scarce.

Entrepreneurship is historically associated with risk bearing. Consequently, risk attitude is widely believed to affect the selection of individuals into entrepreneurial positions. This belief, however, has not yet been put to an empirical test. The objective of Chapter 4 is to provide such a test on a unique sample of Dutch labour force participants. One of the unique aspects of this sample is the availability of a measure of an individual's risk attitude.

The Dutch data support the supposedly negative effect of risk aversion on entrepreneurship selection or venture creation. However, the research does not provide a definitive conclusion on the causality of the relationship between risk attitude and entrepreneurship selection because the empirical measure of risk attitude has some drawbacks.

No matter how important it is to understand the issues and determinants of venture *creation*, the inevitable next question concerns venture *performance*, the topic of Parts III and IV. Business development is a stressful and highly demanding type of activity, which ends in failure and deception in far too many cases (20 per cent of the ventures do not survive their first year; see Fritsch et al., 2004). As indicated in Audretsch and Keilbach (2003), the social costs of business failure are immense, whereas the social benefits of a successful enterprise are enormous in terms of innovation, growth and competition. Hence, devising policy measures stimulating the decrease of barriers to entry for potentially successful starters and the increase of useful support to those starters can have a large impact on the economic development of countries. This is why many countries and international organizations like the European Commission, the International Monetary Fund (IMF) and the World Bank put large amounts of energy into designing and implementing such measures.

The effective design of policy measures to improve successful entrepreneurship requires quantitative knowledge about the determinants of venture performance. It will therefore be based on output from research into such determinants. Part III describes the state of the art of such research and reviews the resulting empirical evidence. It starts with Chapter 5, which provides the link with the earlier chapters.

Chapter 5 develops a theoretical model that explains business formation and labour demand simultaneously. In this manner, the decision to start up as an entrepreneur (Part II) and entrepreneurial (socioeconomic) success (Part III) are analysed within one framework. The explanatory factors are risk attitude and entrepreneurial ability. Whether an active labour force participant becomes an entrepreneur or an employee depends on the utilities associated with each activity. These in turn depend on individual risk attitude, since entrepreneurship is a risky business, and on entrepreneurial talent. Expected entrepreneurial talent determines the potential size of one's business. The actual size of an entrepreneur's firm is dependent on the realized level of his entrepreneurial talent. Entrepreneurial talent is a function of observable characteristics. A measure of relative risk aversion is also observed.

The resulting equilibrium model is translated into an empirical structural model which explains whether one starts a business, and if a business is started how many people one employs. The estimation results pertain to a sample of Dutch individuals. It turns out (again) that more risk-averse individuals are significantly less inclined to become an entrepreneur. Basically, entrepreneurial ability depends on the same set of human capital characteristics that also affects the earnings of an employed individual.

The objective of Chapter 6 is to find the determinants of entrepreneurial success for the group of individuals identified in Chapter 3 as having sufficient willingness and opportunity to start up as an entrepreneur. The chapter quantifies individual-specific determinants of entrepreneurship duration. I distinguish between two exit reasons (or destinations). The (statistically) distinct exit destinations are compulsory and voluntary exits from entrepreneurship. Compulsory exits are seen as indicating a lack of business success.

The empirical results with respect to compulsory exits, that is, business failures, are related to the historical theories of entrepreneurship that are reviewed in Chapter 2. The estimated effects of regressors on hazards differ considerably from their effects on the start-up probability. Hazards are affected by human capital variables but not by one's financial position at the start. General business conditions matter.

Part IV focuses on the two main determinants of venture performance: human and financial capital. The motivation for this focus is fourfold. First, broad research shows that these two factors, human and financial capital, are the main drivers of venture performance (and also of venture development) (see Le, 1999; van Praag, 2003). In general, they are more influential for performance than, for instance, ethnicity, family background, social capital, or the business strategy and organization of the small business starter. Second, the relationship between performance and many of the aforementioned potential determinants, such as business strategy and social capital, is, in turn, determined by the human and financial capital of the entrepreneur. Third, policy interventions relating to these determinants are most straightforward. Finally, the state of the art of the research into these factors is most developed, though certainly not without criticism.

Chapter 7 examines the effect of schooling on entrepreneurship earnings. It compares the rate of return to schooling for entrepreneurs with that for employees. The robust finding is that entrepreneurs benefit more than employees from an additional year of schooling, provided that the effect has been measured such that one copes with possible problems of endogeneity and unobserved heterogeneity.

Chapter 8 relates entrepreneurial profits and duration to capital constraints at the time of inception of the business. It shows that capital constraints do hinder entrepreneurs in their performance. The result is robust against various alternative explanations. Entrepreneurs who have been hindered by capital constraints at their start-up phase (but have nevertheless started!) are unable to follow an optimal scheme of investments in terms of amounts and timing of investment. Therefore, they have more difficulty surviving and their business is less profitable.

Finally, Chapter 9 summarizes the main findings and conclusions of the preceding chapters. Policy recommendations are also discussed in this last chapter.

Notes

1. This is the definition that de Wit uses for self-employed persons and entrepreneurs alike. He motivates why this definition of self-employment and entrepreneurship is appropriate (de Wit, 1993, pp. 2–3).
2. Earnings are of course expressed in the local currency, and they may reflect before- or after-tax values – although it is more likely that business and sales taxes have been accounted for as part of the cost of doing business.
3. A voluntary exit does not necessarily mean a lack of success.

2 Some classic views on entrepreneurship*

> In order to solve the many problems of today both in the private and the public sectors, entrepreneurial activity on a large scale, based on a sensitive and innovative attitude, guided by a broad concept of welfare, is needed even more than before. (Heertje, 1982, p. 91)

Introduction

Given the importance of entrepreneurship in economic practice today, the question readily arises: what is its role in economic theory and how did it develop? In order to answer this question, I shall review some mainstream historical contributions to the theory of entrepreneurship, which started to develop halfway through the eighteenth century.[1]

Historically, philosophers of science did not hold entrepreneurs in high esteem. Entrepreneurs were not at all regarded as enhancing society's well-being. Making a profit, the economic definition of the pecuniary return to entrepreneurship, had been perceived as robbery ever since Aristotle introduced the persistent idea of economic activity as a 'zero-sum-game', that is, one man's gain is another man's loss.

Today, however, scientists and policy makers do acknowledge the importance of the entrepreneur's role in society (see Chapter 1). Thus, economic value is created when potentially unsuccessful start-ups are prevented, or even better, when they are turned into successful ones. Moreover, potentially successful entrepreneurs who do not start, should be motivated and/or offered this opportunity in order to increase economic value. Determinants of entrepreneurial start-up and success can serve as an instrument for gaining insight into the manner in which this value can be enhanced through appropriate policy measures.

To locate potential successful entrepreneurs who are willing and able to start up as an entrepreneur, and to distinguish them from potentially less successful entrepreneurs, I seek an answer to the research question: 'What are the determinants of successful entrepreneurship?'. In this chapter, I shall answer this question from a historical angle by reviewing important historical contributions to the theory of entrepreneurship. The relevant ideas of Richard Cantillon, Jean-Baptiste Say, Alfred Marshall, Joseph Schumpeter, Frank Knight and Israel Kirzner are reviewed below.

Selection of scholars

There are a large number of contributors to the theory of entrepreneurship and space is limited. Therefore, I had to decide which subset of scholars would be reviewed here. Two criteria are applied in this assessment of whether a contributor is 'important'.

First, does the author contribute to the systematic generation of knowledge in the field of entrepreneurship (as determined by satisfying one or more of the following criteria)?

1. Does the author develop a new theory for phenomena not previously explained in the field of entrepreneurship?
2. Does the author falsify a prior theory of entrepreneurship and does he replace it with a new one?
3. Does the author expand the scope of an existing theory of entrepreneurship by showing that it can explain more or different phenomena?
4. Does the author reduce specific theories to more general ones?

Second, has the scholar been important in the sense that his work has directed the thinking of (future) researchers on the topic?

In my opinion, the six authors mentioned meet these two necessary criteria of 'importance' within their own frame of reference.

Selection of research questions

For each of these authors, I shall address the following questions:

1. What is the position of the entrepreneur within the economic system as described by the contributor?
2. What is the entrepreneur's position within the firm?
3. How is the entrepreneurial task defined?
4. What kind of entrepreneurial ability or personality is needed to perform the task successfully?
5. What are the returns on entrepreneurship and what is the entrepreneurial drive?
6. What determines supply and demand in the market for entrepreneurs?

The answers to the first three questions primarily aim at obtaining a definition and understanding of each author's concept of the 'entrepreneur'. Dwelling on the concept itself makes sense, as there are almost as many definitions as there are contributors to the theory of entrepreneurship. Not only have many authors given more meaning to the concept of 'entrepreneur' than have been put forth by their predecessors, but they have also advanced new and often opposing meanings for the term, with or without falsifying the existing notions. Part of the difference in defining the term is caused by the different views on the economic system as a whole. How central is the entrepreneurial function within the different perceived systems? What are the underlying assumptions in the explanation of the system? The answers to these questions play a prominent role in explaining the differing perceptions of the entrepreneur.

The answers to the last three questions result in direct indicators of the determinants of success and of the decision to start up as an entrepreneur.

The earliest thought on entrepreneurship

Richard Cantillon (1680?–1734) was the earliest scholar to pay considerable attention to the entrepreneur. Indeed, he introduced the very concept of 'entrepreneur',[2] and he was the first to acknowledge that there is an entrepreneurial function within the economic system. Thereafter, as in Cantillon's (posthumous) publication *Essai sur la nature du commerce en général* in 1755, entrepreneurs would appear in economic theory as contributors to society's economic value.

In his economic system, Cantillon recognizes three types of agents: (i) landowners (capitalists); (ii) entrepreneurs (arbitragers); and (iii) hirelings (wage workers). His perception of the market is one of a 'self-regulating network of reciprocal exchange arrangements'. The entrepreneur has a central role in this system because he is responsible for all the exchange and circulation in the economy.[3] The class of entrepreneurs brings about the equilibrium of supply and demand.

The entrepreneurial class accomplishes its task by engaging in pure arbitrage. The motivating factor is the potential profit generated from the activity of 'buying at a certain price and selling at an uncertain price'.[4] Cantillon thus recognizes that arbitrage always involves uncertainty. His entrepreneurs also engage in professional activities other than arbitrage (the farmer, the transporter, the banker or the seller in the marketplace, for instance). The distinguishing feature of the entrepreneurial task as compared to the other types of agents is its risk-bearing nature, which yields uncertain and non-contractually arranged incomes.[5] Landowners and hirelings are not subject to uncertain incomes, the former because of their rents, which are fixed by contract, the latter because of their fixed wages.

As the entrepreneur's task basically comprises arbitrage, he should be alert and forward looking but need not be innovative. He adjusts the quantity supplied to existing demand; he does not increase or alter either demand or total supply. And the entrepreneur should be well prepared to bear the inherent risk. An entrepreneur, though, does not necessarily start his venture backed by his own capital. Capital can be borrowed on the (assumed perfect) money market by paying the price of borrowing (interest) to the banker, another entrepreneurial profession.[6]

The laws of demand and supply also determine the number of entrepreneurs in each occupation. If there are too many wine merchants, some of them will go bankrupt until the surplus disappears. This adjustment process will not take place at random but according to the 'survival of the fittest' principle: the worst-equipped merchants will go bankrupt.[7] On the other hand, if there are too few entrepreneurs, new ones will be attracted by the advantages of enterprise.

In summary, Cantillon was the first to give economic meaning to the concept of 'entrepreneur'. The entrepreneur is functionally described as an arbitrager. By engaging in arbitrage and bearing risk, the entrepreneurial class has an equilibrating function within the economic system. The prerequisite for the existence of an entrepreneurial class is uncertainty.

A classical thought on entrepreneurship

In Jean-Baptiste Say's (1767–1832) *A Treatise on Political Economy or the Production, Distribution and Consumption of Wealth* ([1803] 1971), the entrepreneur plays a central coordinating role in both production and distribution. Also within the firm, he is the coordinator and, moreover, the modern leader and manager. Say is the first economist to stress this managerial role for the entrepreneur. Compared to other classical economists, he gives a very prominent position to the entrepreneur in the entire system of production and consumption. He extends the entrepreneurial function as defined by Cantillon. However, by treating entrepreneurship mainly as a superior kind of labour, 'Say consciously or unconsciously directed attention away from the uniqueness of the entrepreneurial role' (Hébert and Link, 1988, p. 34).

Say's theory of the entrepreneur in fact arises from his *explicit* rejection of the 'zero-sum game' economy: 'They all take it for granted, that what one individual gains must need be lost to another . . . As if the possessions of abundance of individuals and of communities could not be multiplied, without the robbery of somebody or other' (Say [1803] 1971, p. 70). Instead, production gives existing materials (capital and nature) a utility they did not possess before. So there is a creation of utility which Say calls the 'production of wealth'. There are three types of industry that can create value: (i) the agricultural industry; (ii) the manufacturing industry; and (iii) the commercial industry. The working of each of these 'human' industries consists of three distinct operations that are seldom performed by one person: (a) theoretical knowledge construction; (b) the application of knowledge; and (c) execution.

Within this division, 'the application of knowledge to the creation of a product for human consumption' (ibid., p. 330) is the entrepreneur's occupation. This 'superior kind of labour' is necessary to set industries in motion and thereby attain prosperity within a country. Theoretical knowledge, as important as it is, easily flows from one nation to another since this diffusion is in the interest of the men of science: 'But there is no way of dispensing with the other two operations of industry . . . so that a country well stocked with intelligent merchants, manufacturers, and agriculturists has more powerful means of attaining prosperity' (ibid., p. 82). The entrepreneur function within the distribution sector is to gather the revenues from the products sold and to distribute these among the several production inputs: labour from the other classes of operation, capital and natural agents. Those inputs are paid a remuneration according to their efforts in the form of wages, interest and rent, respectively.

The entrepreneur has a key position within his own enterprise; he is the coordinator, modern leader and manager. However, the entrepreneur should perform tasks specific to the trade as well and he will (most of the time) also supply (at least part of) his own capital. He is a risk bearer as well: 'there is a chance of failure pertaining to any entrepreneur activity, however well conducted. The entrepreneur may then lose fortune and in some measure his character' (ibid., p. 331).

A successful entrepreneur should have many qualities. The combination of the various tasks 'requires a combination of moral qualities that are not often found together. Judgement, perseverance, and a knowledge of the world as well as of business . . . the art of superintendence and administration' (ibid., pp. 330–31). Furthermore, a successful entrepreneur should have experience within, and knowledge of, the occupation and be in a position to provide the necessary funds:

> Not that he should be already rich; for he may work upon borrowed capital; but he must at least be solvent, and have the reputation of intelligence, prudence, probity and regularity; and must be able by the nature of his connexions, to procure the loan of capital he may happen himself not to possess. (ibid., pp. 330–31)

The number of competitors in the entrepreneurial market is limited due to the requisite characteristics, talent and capacity. The limited supply maintains the price of successful entrepreneurial labour at a high level, since in Say's classical economy all prices are determined by supply and demand. 'Thus, it is this class of producers, which accumulates the largest fortunes, whenever the productive exertion is crowned by unusual success' (ibid., p. 332).

At the micro level of the firm, the entrepreneur's remuneration is determined as a residual payment: turnover minus the payments to the other inputs of the production process. If this residual is higher than the wage for management and some risk premium, implying positive profits, then the supply of entrepreneurs increases. If profits are negative, then firms go bankrupt until equilibrium prevails.

In summary, the entrepreneur plays a pivotal role in Say's theory of production, distribution and consumption. He is a coordinator both on the market level as well as on the firm level. He is the modern leader and manager within his firm. The successful entrepreneur needs a rare combination of qualities and experiences. Therefore, the number of competitors on the market for entrepreneurs is limited. Consequently, the residual income of the firm when the market is in equilibrium or the entrepreneurial wage can become very high.

A neoclassical thought on entrepreneurship

A general point of view

Early neoclassical economists, mainly represented by A. Marshall (1842–1924), F.Y. Edgeworth (1845–1926) and A.C. Pigou (1877–1959), paid considerable attention to the theory of entrepreneurship. However, the formalized models of the majority of later neoclassical economists did not substantially contribute to the theory of entrepreneurship.[8] As these models have heavily influenced current research methods, especially in microeconomics and also in entrepreneurship, the 'textbook' neoclassical school of thought is introduced here briefly.

In the usual interpretation of the neoclassical model, all individual agents have perfect information and have their economic objectives clearly stated. Firms choose profit-maximizing production bundles, given their production function. In choosing levels of input, the firm performs a calculation, which yields optimal values for all of its decision variables, and these values constitute the profit-maximizing business decision. Consumers choose consumption bundles so as to maximize their expected utility levels, given their budgets. In equilibrium, there is one set of prices at which demand for each good equals supply of that good (production plus initial endowments). All markets (which are implicitly assumed to exist and to work perfectly well) are cleared at this set of equilibrium prices. The optimal values remain unchanged until there is an exogenous change in the economic environment. Then the calculations are repeated and new values are set and remain valid until a new shock occurs. Attention is focused on equilibrium results, achieved in a world without uncertainty. The dynamic adjustment process towards equilibrium is certainly underexplored. Moreover, since credit markets work perfectly well, internal supply of capital is not necessary.

The neoclassical model, with its production function, the logic of rational choice and perfect information, leaves no room for an active entrepreneur. The firm runs itself. The entrepreneur has vanished.[9]

> Obviously, the entrepreneur has been read out of the model. There is no room for enterprise or initiative. The management group becomes a passive calculator. One hears of no . . . brilliant innovations, of no charisma or any of the other stuff of which entrepreneurship is made; one does not hear of them because there is no way in which they can fit into the model. The model is essentially an instrument of optimality analysis of well-defined problems which need no entrepreneur for their solution. (Baumol, 1968, p. 67 and also 1993, p. 13)

The mainstream modern neoclassicists have apparently not cared to include the entrepreneur in their formalized model. However, earlier neoclassical theories paid considerable attention to the entrepreneur (before the 1930s). Marshall's seminal work *Principles of Economics*, first published in 1890, shows that the entrepreneur was important in neoclassical thought. Marshall's theory attached a more prominent role to the entrepreneur than any other early neoclassical theory.

Marshall's point of view
In a Marshallian society, the entrepreneur's task is the supply of commodities and at the same time (as a byproduct) the provision of innovations and progress. Marshall illustrates the importance of innovations: 'Those businessmen who have pioneered new paths have often conferred on society benefits out of all proportion to their own gains, even though they have died millionaires' (Marshall [1890] 1930, p.598). Businesses that benefit society most are not necessarily the firms that will survive within the competitive Marshallian environment. The reward of every business undertaker is proportionate to the direct (private), rather than to the indirect (social) benefits he renders to society (ibid., p. 598).

Within the firm, the entrepreneur bears all the responsibility and exercises all control. He directs production, undertakes business risks, he coordinates capital and labour, and he is both manager and employer. The alert entrepreneur continuously seeks opportunities (that is, innovations) to minimize costs for a given result.

Consequently, successful entrepreneurship obviously requires specific skills and capacities. First, general ability (as opposed to specialized ability) and intelligence are required to enable one to attain great success in any pursuit and especially in business. General ability implies:

> [Being] able to bear in mind many things at a time, to have everything ready when wanted, to act promptly and show resource when anything goes wrong, to accommodate oneself quickly to changes, to be steady and trustworthy, to have always a reserve of force ... (Ibid., pp. 206–7).

This general ability depends on family background, education and innate ability. Second, successful entrepreneurship requires specialized abilities such as knowledge of the trade, power of forecasting, of seeing where there is an opportunity and of undertaking risks. Third, to perform his role as an employer, the entrepreneur should be a 'natural leader of men' (ibid., p. 298).

Not only are these abilities required to make a successful entrepreneur; good fortune as well as business opportunities are also necessary requirements. The opportunity of acquiring the capital required to allow ability to be effectively utilized differs among people. In any event, people working with borrowed capital have a disadvantage over those who have capital themselves. If the businessman working on borrowed capital is less successful, lenders can easily draw back their loans. Consequently, one misfortune may lead to another far more rapidly. Sons of entrepreneurs have additional advantages over others when starting a business. And these advantages are not restricted to their father's trade. The son of an entrepreneur has more business opportunities because he has experienced from his youth the proceedings of a real business.

The returns to entrepreneurship differ from those in other branches of labour. Individual profits show a much higher variance than do ordinary earnings. The number of successful entrepreneurs is but a small percentage of the whole. Moreover, entrepreneurs earn a rent on the rare abilities required for their tasks. These rents may be regarded as an especially important element in the incomes of businessmen – a surplus.

Apart from the level of expected earnings, there are other factors which may affect the decision to start up a business. The difficulty and stress of the work and the variance of earnings will usually have a negative effect on the decision, 'though a few extremely high prices have a disproportionately great attractive force' (ibid., p. 554). The latter phenomenon occurs because (young) risk lovers are more attracted by the prospect of great success than they are deterred by the fear of failure. These rarely experienced high incomes make entrepreneurship stand out as a position of high esteem, which also constitutes a great attraction.

Entrepreneurial supply is constrained by the abilities required for it. Therefore, the entrepreneurial supply price, as determined by the equilibrating forces of supply and demand, is high. And as long as entrepreneurial profits (net advantages) are higher than the earnings in other occupations, and as long as there are still people with the required abilities and enough opportunity, fresh businessmen enter into the trade. If there are too many businessmen in command of capital to sustain the high price, the 'survival of the fittest' principle, referred to by Marshall as the 'substitution' principle, determines who remains in the trade and who exits.

In brief, the Marshallian market economy centres on the entrepreneurial class. Entrepreneurs drive the production and distribution process: they coordinate supply and demand on the market, and capital and labour within the firm. They undertake all the risks that are associated with production. They lead and manage their firms. They are cost minimizers and are therefore also innovators and the cause of progress. The abilities required are many and combinations of them are scarce in society. Consequently, the supply price for entrepreneurship will generally be high.

Entrepreneurship and Schumpeter
Joseph Schumpeter (1883–1950) contributed significantly to the theory of entrepreneurship. Most of his ideas are reflected in his book *The Theory of Economic Development*, first published in 1911. His theory was the first to treat innovation as an endogenous process. He turned down the predominant paradigm of entrepreneurship as management of the firm and replaced it with an alternative one: the entrepreneur as leader of the firm (in modern business management language) and as the innovator and, therefore, prime mover of the economic system. Schumpeter integrated the dynamics of technology and business enterprise by defining the entrepreneur as an innovator. He explicitly opposed the idea of the entrepreneur as a risk bearer and a capitalist. He integrated psychological theory into the economic theory of entrepreneurship.

To describe the entrepreneur's contribution to the economy, Schumpeter starts his theory with a contrasting world: one without the entrepreneur, 'the circular flow'. In this static world, every day is a repetition of the preceding one. It is a world without uncertainty or change. All decisions can be taken unconsciously upon long experience: 'In this model . . . all the alternatives have been explored and compared, so that for every matter that was to be decided, the optimal choice has been adopted' (Baumol, 1993, p. 5). Then the entrepreneur appears on stage. He seeks opportunities for profit. He introduces 'new combinations' or innovations to reach this goal.[10] Schumpeter sees this innovative creation of the entrepreneur as the prime endogenous cause of change (development) in the economic system. New entrepreneurial combinations destroy the equilibrium in the economy (in the circular flow) and create a new one. Ongoing innovation therefore implies permanent (discontinuous) change and permanent disequilibrium.

An entrepreneur is not necessarily the director and independent owner of a business. An entrepreneur is a person who introduces new combinations, in whatever position.[11] Generally, new combinations are not implemented by the producers of the combinations they (will eventually) replace. As a rule they are embodied in new firms that start producing alongside the old firms. Thus, old firms are eliminated whenever they cease to introduce new combinations themselves.[12] The entrepreneur's task is to innovate and to lead, that is, deciding which objectives to pursue rather than deciding on how to pursue them. He is not a risk bearer or a supplier of capital. Both of these tasks are left to the banker.

Being apt and willing to take up an entrepreneurial task requires a rare attitude and a particular conduct. Leadership is required in order to 'lead' existing means of production into new channels (out of the accustomed ones). Moreover, the entrepreneur should not feel reluctant to do something new: 'This mental freedom . . . is something peculiar and by nature rare' (Schumpeter [1911] 1939, p. 86). By doing something new and thereby showing deviating behaviour, opposition arises in the social environment. The entrepreneur should 'be strong enough to swim against the tide of the society in which he is living' (Heertje, 1982, p. 86). Furthermore, innovating requires some special psychological motives.[13] Entrepreneurs do not perform their task in the first place in order to satisfy their own consumption wants. The motivating factors of pursuing indirect instead of direct consumption are:

- the dream and will to found a private kingdom in order to achieve social distinction. This dream is the more fascinating, the less opportunity for achieving social distinction is available to an individual;
- the will to conquer, to fight, to prove oneself superior to others, to succeed for the sake of success itself, not of the fruits of success; and
- the joy of creation, of getting things done, to exercise energy, to change for the joy of changing.

It is not necessary to be rich to have the opportunity to start up as an entrepreneur. Innovations can be equally well supported by own wealth as by credits. If they are supported by own wealth, the entrepreneur fulfils two jobs: that of the entrepreneur and that of the banker. Anyhow, it is the banker who bears the financial risk pertaining to an innovation, not the entrepreneur.

Implementing innovations is a profit-driven activity. However, most entrepreneurs are not motivated by the purchasing power provided by profit, but rather aim at business success for which profit is an indicator. 'By being the first to introduce a "new combination", the entrepreneur obtains temporary monopoly power' (Baumol, 1993, p. 6). But profit is the signal to imitators that above normal gains can be made. Hence, entry and competition erode the initial profit position of the entrepreneur sooner or later and a new equilibrium position is reached: 'Even if the entrepreneur succeeds in establishing a monopoly whose returns continue indefinitely . . . the flow of gains to the entrepreneur *in her entrepreneurial* role must be very temporary. . . . It is transformed into monopoly rent rather than entrepreneurial profit' (ibid., p. 7).

Hence, being an entrepreneur is neither a profession, nor a lasting condition. Entrepreneurs do not form a social class, though successful entrepreneurship may lead to certain class positions, according to how the proceeds of the business are used. This class position is also part of the remuneration of the entrepreneur. It can be maintained for several generations by the inheritance of pecuniary results and entrepreneurial qualities. This makes further enterprise easier for descendants, though they cannot inherit the entrepreneurial position itself. The rare motivating forces required for it largely restrict entrepreneurial supply.

To sum up, Schumpeter's entrepreneur is an innovator and a leader. But he is not a risk bearer, or a manager or a capitalist. The innovator is the engine of growth of Schumpeter's economy. He leads the economy away from its (otherwise static) equilibrium position and forces it to a higher equilibrium position. Innovations are endogenous developments in Schumpeter's dynamic economic system. Entrepreneurs are willing to innovate, due to the possession of some scarce motivating forces. Neither entrepreneurial activity nor profit is lasting. Entrepreneurship is a temporary condition for any person, unless he keeps on innovating.

Entrepreneurship and Knight

Frank Knight's (1885–1972) major contributions to the theory of entrepreneurship are included in his doctoral dissertation *Risk, Uncertainty and Profit*, first published in 1921. He was the first to distinguish explicitly between risk and (true) uncertainty. The economic function of the entrepreneur is bearing the real uncertainty. Knight has generalized Cantillon's theory of entrepreneurship. The entrepreneur bears uncertainty (more specifically defined than Cantillon's risk), and entrepreneurship involves more than arbitrage only. Moreover, Knight has contributed a thorough analysis of the motivations and characteristics needed to become a successful entrepreneur, a successful uncertainty bearer and judgemental decision maker.

The characteristic feature of the society through which the entrepreneur acquires his role is uncertainty. Uncertainty, unlike risk, comprises a type of probability for which there is no valid basis at all for classifying instances because it concerns the outcome of a unique event. Hence, judgement should be exercised for both the formation of an estimate and the estimation of its value. This true uncertainty forms the basis of Knight's theory of profit, competition and entrepreneurship and had previously been ignored in economic theory. It is borne by a particular subset of individuals in society: the entrepreneurs:

> The work of forecasting and at the same time a large part of the technological direction and control of production are still further concentrated upon a very narrow class of the producers, and we meet with a new economic functionary, the entrepreneur. (Knight [1921] 1971, p. 268)

Business decisions practically never concern calculable probabilities. Entrepreneurs are specialized in responsible direction and control, in dealing with real uncertainty, while all others furnish them with productive services for which the entrepreneur guarantees a fixed remuneration. Thus, entrepreneurs assume the uncertainty of changing consumer wants or changing purchasing power. The savings resulting from reducing uncertainty accrue to society (ibid., pp. 278–9). Entrepreneurs are held responsible for economic progress, like improvements in technology and business organization. It is extremely important and lucrative to society to select individuals who are most apt for entrepreneurial positions. Entrepreneurial ability is the bottleneck in determining the size of each business.

The essence of the entrepreneur's position in a corporation is his responsibility for direction and control whenever uncertainty is involved. He exercises judgement effectively, is the decision maker, and he takes the responsibility for his decisions. Decisions include the planning of where, when and what kind of capital goods to create. In addition to these estimating and judicial tasks, the entrepreneur is responsible for guaranteeing the estimated values to the other parties involved with his firm. The entrepreneur assumes the uninsurable business hazard.[14]

Successful entrepreneurship requires not only entrepreneurial ability (as described below) but also good luck and the belief in one's good fortune. Entrepreneurial ability is heavily dependent on one's ability to deal with uncertainty effectively. Differences among individuals with respect to their ability to deal with uncertainty, cause the entrepreneur's function to be specialized in the hands of those who are most able to deal with it. The power to deal with uncertainty effectively requires the following: a high degree of self-confidence, the power to judge one's own personal qualities as compared to those of other individuals (competitors, suppliers, buyers and employees), a disposition to act on one's own opinion, venturesomeness and foresight.[15] Furthermore, entrepreneurial ability includes, besides the requirements for dealing with uncertainty, 'the power of effective control over other men as well as the intellectual capacity to decide what should be done' (ibid., p. 269). In addition, success as an entrepreneur depends on the availability of enough capital to guarantee factors their fixed remunerations. As long as a prospective entrepreneur believes in his own capacity and has the wealth to back up his judgement, he does not need to convince others in order to dispose of the necessary capital for starting a business. But if he is not wealthy enough, he should find some external financial backing and hence, be able to convince this outside party of the correctness of his judgements.

The entrepreneurial task is rewarded with the residual income, that is, profit, the reward for bearing uncertainty. The competition of (prospective) entrepreneurs bidding in the market for society's productive services determines prices:

> The division of social income between profits and contractual income then depends upon the supply of entrepreneur ability in the society and the rapidity of diminishing returns from (other factors applied to) it, the size of the profit share increasing as the supply of ability is small and as the returns diminish more rapidly. . . . The size of the profit share depends on whether entrepreneurs tend on the whole to overestimate or underestimate the prospects of business operations, being larger if they underestimate. (Ibid., pp. 284–5)

The income of any particular entrepreneur will tend to be larger with higher ability and more good luck, given the division of social income and its underlying factors as given above. The Knightian entrepreneur is not only remunerated with profit; the prestige of entrepreneurship and the satisfaction resulting from being one's own boss should also be considered when studying entrepreneurial income.

Finally, the number of entrepreneurs operating in the market depends, as competition is assumed, upon the demand and supply of entrepreneurial services. Demand for entrepreneurs depends directly upon the supply of other productive services and on the ability of individual entrepreneurs. And,

> The supply of entrepreneurs involves the factors of (a) ability, with the various elements therein included, (b) willingness, (c) power to give satisfactory guarantees, and (d) the coincidence of these factors. Willingness plus power to give guarantees, not backed up by ability, will evidently lead to a dissipation of resources, while ability without the other two factors will be merely wasted. (Ibid., pp. 282–3)

In summary, the Knightian entrepreneur contributes savings to society by bearing all the uncertainty: he makes decisions for which he is responsible. He guarantees the factors of production their fixed remuneration. Entrepreneurship requires the ability to bear uncertainty as well as the availability of enough capital to pay the remunerations, which have been guaranteed. Entrepreneurial services are remunerated by profit, a residual payment, but also by prestige and job satisfaction. The amount of profit any particular entrepreneur makes, increases with his own ability and good luck and decreases with the degree of self-confidence that entrepreneurs have as a group. Entrepreneurial services are supplied if an individual is willing and possesses sufficient capital.

A neo-Austrian thought on entrepreneurship

A general point of view
The Austrian view of the market economy is one that differs significantly from the standard view of economists. Neoclassicists analyse the market in a state of (general) equilibrium. Neo-Austrians consider it most unlikely that the market economy is close to a general equilibrium position at any time. They try to answer the question of how, if at all, market economies tend towards equilibrium. Neo-Austrians see such tendencies as arising out of the dynamics of discovery. Such discovery identifies opportunities for pure profit, which express, in turn, errors stemming from 'utter ignorance', that is, unawareness of a basic lack of information.

Kirzner's point of view
Kirzner gave the entrepreneur a pivotal position within the market process. Most of his ideas relating to the entrepreneur can be found in his publication *Competition and Entrepreneurship* (1973):

> One of our complaints concerning contemporary theories of price arises from their virtual elimination of entrepreneurship. What is required, I have argued, is a reformulation of price theory to readmit the entrepreneurial role to its rightful position as crucial to the very operation of the market. (Ibid., p. 75)

Kirzner has clearly contributed to the Austrian mode of thinking as well as to the theory of entrepreneurship by stating that entrepreneurs are those people in the economy who are alert to discover and exploit profit opportunities. They are, according to Kirzner, the equilibrating force in the market process.

The equilibrium position itself is still never reached; entrepreneurs may have erred in their assessments concerning the presence of profit opportunities or may have completely overlooked them. Such errors are translated, in turn, into new opportunities for pure entrepreneurial gain (and new errors in turn). Moreover, even successful entrepreneurial endeavours proceed against the background of spontaneously changing underlying conditions of supply and demand; such changes alter what needs to be discovered. Profit opportunities include making a profit out of (i) buying (selling) at one place and selling (buying) at another; (ii) buying in one period and selling in another; and/or (iii) buying inputs and selling modified outputs.

Hence, entrepreneurs are likely to be producers as well. However, producers or others are entrepreneurs only if they make discoveries and if they also make a profit out of these discoveries. Production takes place within the firm. But,

> The firm, then, is that which results *after* the entrepreneur has completed some entrepreneurial decision-making, specifically the purchase of certain resources. . . . The particular entrepreneur is no longer only a pure entrepreneur; he has become, as a result of earlier entrepreneurial decisions, an owner of resources. (Ibid., pp. 52–3)

Kirzner's entrepreneur requires no special ability or personality to carry out his function: the pure entrepreneur could even hire all the required labour and business talent. Entrepreneurship requires, however, a very special type of knowledge:

> The kind of knowledge required for entrepreneurship is 'knowing where to look for knowledge'. . . . The word, which captures most closely this kind of 'knowledge', seems to be *alertness*. It is true that 'alertness' too may be hired; but one who hires an employee alert to possibilities of discovering knowledge has himself displayed knowledge of a still higher order. Entrepreneurial knowledge may be described as the 'highest order of knowledge'. (Ibid., p. 68)

The entrepreneur only needs to perceive profit opportunities in an earlier stage than others. He needs to be alert. Entrepreneurs are the most alert persons to profit opportunities in the economy. They have, more than average, the ability to learn from mistakes in the sense of not perceiving the best opportunities. Exploiting profit opportunities, as opposed to discovering them, requires some additional characteristics. However, exploitation is not the entrepreneurial act itself.

Once a profit opportunity has been discovered, one 'can capture the associated profits by innovating, changing and creating' (ibid., p. 67). Hence, to be able to act upon a profit opportunity appropriately requires additional qualities such as creativeness and leadership.

Entrepreneurship is not restricted to persons who own resources themselves. A profit opportunity may require the investment of capital, 'But it is still correct to insist that the entrepreneur qua entrepreneur requires no investment of any kind' (ibid., p. 49). Capitalists advance necessary funds as long as the entrepreneur is in a position to finance the necessary interest payments. Kirzner's entrepreneur, however, still bears some uncertainty:

> The longer the time before the venture's required outlay can be expected to bring the hoped-for revenues, the less sure of himself the entrepreneur is likely to be. The entrepreneurial activity (as described here) undoubtedly involves uncertainty and the bearing of risk. (Ibid., p. 78)

Discovery is not accidental, but is inspired by the prospect of (entrepreneurial) profit. Entrepreneurial actions reflect these profit-inspired discoveries. Hence, entrepreneurs are likely to be the most alert persons either by nature, or because the profit incentive is more important to them than to others.

Summing up, it is the systematic sequence of error (in the entrepreneurial assessment of profit opportunities), profit opportunity, discovery and correction that constitutes the market process. It is a process, which, in the light of continually changing supply and demand conditions, never ceases. This market process, in which the entrepreneur plays a predominant role as alert discoverer of profit opportunities, is responsible for the short-run movement of prices and production decisions, as well as for long-term progress and growth. Such an entrepreneurial market process is, at the same time, a competitive process in the sense that it relies on the freedom of potential entrepreneurs to enter markets in order to compete for perceived available profits.

A comparison

The following summarizes the answers to the six research questions by each of the six authors reviewed in the chapter.

1. What is the position of the entrepreneur within the economic system as described by the contributor?

   - Cantillon   arbitrager who establishes equilibrium
   - Say   coordinator of production and distribution
   - Marshall   supplier of commodities (and innovation and progress)
   - Schumpeter   creative destructor of equilibrium, engine of growth
   - Knight   bearer of the 'real' uncertainty, cause of progress
   - Kirzner   agent causing tendency towards equilibrium (never reached)

2. What is the entrepreneur's position within the firm?

   - Cantillon   no statement
   - Say   leader, manager and coordinator
   - Marshall   employer, manager and coordinator
   - Schumpeter   the one who introduces new combinations

- Knight   to direct, control and make decisions when uncertainty is involved, responsible for guaranteeing a fixed remuneration to factors of production
- Kirzner   the firm's existence results from entrepreneurial decision making

3. How is the entrepreneurial task defined?

- Cantillon   arbitrage and risk bearing
- Say   application of knowledge, experiment and bear the inherent risk
- Marshall   to control, to bear responsibility and risk
- Schumpeter to seek profit opportunities, to decide which objectives to pursue, to introduce new combinations
- Knight   to assume the uninsurable business hazard
- Kirzner   to discover and exploit profit opportunities

4. What kind of entrepreneurial ability or personality is needed to perform the task successfully?

- Cantillon   alertness and foresight
- Say   rare combination of qualities and experiences
- Marshall   'general' and specialized ability, leadership and good luck
- Schumpeter willingness to show deviating behaviour and leadership
- Knight   being able to deal with uncertainty, power of effective control, belief in one's good luck and (ability to obtain) capital
- Kirzner   alertness: the knowledge of where to look for knowledge

5. What are the returns on entrepreneurship and what is the entrepreneurial drive?

- Cantillon   potential profit
- Say   high 'wage' rate plus risk premium
- Marshall   high 'wage' rate with high variance, attracting risk lovers, high esteem
- Schumpeter success measured by profit, social distinction, the joy of creation
- Knight   profit, prestige, satisfaction from being one's own boss
- Kirzner   profit

6.   What determines supply and demand in the market for entrepreneurs?

- Cantillon   laws of supply and demand, 'survival of the fittest'
- Say   as above (Cantillon), plus limited supply due to scarcity of abilities required
- Marshall   as above (Say)
- Schumpeter   supply restricted by rare motivating forces required
- Knight   laws of supply and demand; supply depends on the number of persons with entrepreneurial ability and ability to obtain capital
- Kirzner   toughness of competition for perceived available profits

Cantillon, Schumpeter and Kirzner all explicitly give an essential role to the entrepreneur as a mover of the market in a certain direction as compared to its equilibrium position. Cantillon's entrepreneur establishes equilibrium. Schumpeter's entrepreneur destroys equilibrium and initiates a movement to a higher equilibrium position. Kirzner's entrepreneur, on the contrary, achieves tendencies towards an equilibrium position that is never realized. The entrepreneur's contribution to the economy perceived by Cantillon, Knight and Kirzner results from the assumption of imperfect information, in one way or another. Cantillon's entrepreneur is the one who deals with risk, Knight's with 'true' uncertainty and Kirzner's with 'utter ignorance'. All the economists except Cantillon attribute economic progress and innovation to the entrepreneur's activities.

Cantillon does not have a clear statement about the relationship between the entrepreneur and the firm. This is perhaps a reflection of the spirit of his time. The theories of entrepreneurship of Say, Marshall and Knight are compatible with the entrepreneur in the position of independent owner, decision maker and manager of the firm. Schumpeter includes the modern 'intrapreneurs' (employees who are in a position to 'carry out new combinations') in his definition of entrepreneur and excludes those business owners who cease to introduce new combinations. In Kirzner's opinion, the firm results after the entrepreneur has completed some entrepreneurial decision making, specifically the purchase of certain resources.

The various descriptions of the entrepreneur's main tasks partly overlap. All but Schumpeter's entrepreneurs are responsible for risk bearing. Cantillon's entrepreneur bears risk as a consequence of selling (buying) at a certain price and buying (selling) at an uncertain price. Say's entrepreneur bears the risk of losing capital and reputation due to experimenting and the chance of failure. The Marshallian entrepreneur is responsible for undertaking the business risk associated with the activities of his firm. Schumpeter explicitly excludes risk bearing from the business of the entrepreneur. Knight, on the contrary, defines the entrepreneur as the decision maker whenever uncertainty is involved. The activity of Kirzner's entrepreneur involves uncertainty: he does not know when and to what extent the expected revenue can be collected. Say and Marshall allocate management (of personnel) to the entrepreneurial task. Knight does so too, but to a lesser extent.

The degree of accessibility of capital markets for entrepreneurs differs among the economic theories reviewed. Cantillon's entrepreneur can borrow the capital required for his venture on the (assumed perfect) money market. Say assumes a capital market with imperfect and asymmetric information. The entrepreneur can borrow money on this market if and only if he has a certain reputation. The Marshallian entrepreneur seems to be able to borrow money on the 'perfect' capital market easily. But the entrepreneur working on borrowed capital has a disadvantage in the operation of his venture: he needs to pay an additional risk premium to compensate the banker for his 'personal' risk. Schumpeter explicitly excludes the supply of capital from the business of the entrepreneur. This implies the assumption of the perfect working of capital markets. The capital market in Knight's economy is far from perfect. Entrepreneurs need wealth; at least enough to pay production factors their guaranteed remuneration. However, Knight acknowledges the possibility of the entrepreneur being able to convince a banker of the correctness of his judgements in order to borrow the capital required. The latest economist reviewed, Kirzner, agrees with Schumpeter in this respect.

The economists' definitions of the entrepreneur's task and position in the economy diverge considerably. This is reflected in their opinions about the capability, conduct and attitude required for the entrepreneur to be successful. Cantillon and Kirzner stress the importance of alertness and foresight, of being able to discover profit opportunities. Say and Marshall give much weight to certain abilities related to management, leadership and industry. Schumpeter supposes successful entrepreneurship to be dependent on a certain attitude, a willingness to show deviating behaviour. Knight integrates psychological requirements in the (neo)classical ability requirements.

Profit is included in all six theories as a return on entrepreneurship, the drive to undertake the task, though Say and Marshall call this a wage. Marshall also includes a high esteem associated with (successful) entrepreneurship in the returns on this 'profession'. According to Schumpeter, profit itself is not the driving force for an entrepreneur, but it is rather the success which can be measured by profit and social distinction. Moreover, he assumes that the joy of creation is a drive in itself. Knight also gives weight to 'psychological' rewards.

The laws of demand and supply mostly determine the amount of entrepreneurship supplied to the market. Entry occurs when above-normal profit levels are realized. The 'survival of the fittest' principle determines who leaves the market when the outlook of profit levels is not too bright. Say and Marshall explain the relatively high wages for entrepreneurs by a limited supply due to the high qualifications for entrance with respect to ability. Supply of entrepreneurs is also restricted in Schumpeter's economy. One needs a scarce combination of motivating forces to become an entrepreneur. According to Knight, supply is restricted due to the limited number of persons who have the willingness combined with command over the capital required to become an entrepreneur.

The answers to the six research questions developed in this chapter lead to a more thorough understanding of the entrepreneur, entrepreneurial success and the important issues in empirical research in this field. Unfortunately, it is impossible to define empirically the concepts 'entrepreneur' and 'entrepreneurial success' in any of the ways the abovementioned authors did. Consequently, the theoretical definitions of these concepts in this chapter do not correspond with the definitions in the empirical chapters. However, acknowledging this, as far as possible I shall integrate the knowledge and understanding obtained in this chapter into the empirical studies that follow. Moreover, where possible, I shall empirically put to the test several ingredients of the six theories with respect to the determinants of (successful) entrepreneurship.

Tables 2.1 and 2.2 are meant to facilitate the integration of these classical theories into the empirical analyses. Table 2.1 contains the empirically testable ingredients of the six theories with respect to the determinants of (successful) entrepreneurship. Determinants of entry into entrepreneurship (column 1) are distinguished from determinants of success (column 2), whenever possible. The distinction is not possible when an author assumes a characteristic to be important for 'successful entrepreneurship'. Determinants of being a successful entrepreneur are found in the third column of Table 2.1.

The classic determinants of successful entrepreneurship in Table 2.1 are often defined in such a way that they are not directly comparable to determinants available from empirical research. Therefore, Table 2.2 translates, as far as possible, the determinants of successful entrepreneurship as defined by the authors reviewed to empirically testable equivalents. These will be used throughout the book (often in combination with factors affecting entrepreneurship that stem from other theoretical sources).

Table 2.1   Empirically testable parts of the six entrepreneurship theories

	Start	Success	Being successful
Cantillon	–	–	Willingness to bear risk
Say	(Sufficient reputation to obtain) capital	Knowledge of the world, business and occupation	Motivation and ability to bear risk
Marshall	(Young) risk lovers	Intelligence, general ability, dependent on: family background, education and innate ability Knowledge of the trade Ability to bear risk Leadership Own capital	Father entrepreneur
Schumpeter	Willingness is higher if: less alternative opportunity for social distinction More ambition	–	Leadership
Knight	Ability to obtain capital Willingness	Ability to deal with uncertainty Intellectual capacity Self-confidence	Certain industries ('basic wants')
Kirzner	–	Leadership	–

Conclusion

The topic of entrepreneurship currently experiences a revived interest as is shown by the research agenda of today's empirical researchers. There are few issues in economics that are backed up by such a rich historical knowledge base, as is the case with entrepreneurship. The danger of forgetting this knowledge base was evoked by a temporary disappearance of the entrepreneur from the theoretical and empirical research agenda. This knowledge base should be considered in current empirical entrepreneurship research. The aim of this chapter has been to give a concise overview of the most important historical contributions relating to today's empirical

Table 2.2 *Translating theoretical into empirical determinants of successful entrepreneurship**

Empirical determinants	Say	Marshall	Schumpeter	Knight
Risk aversion	Bear risk	Ability to bear risk	–	Ability to deal with uncertainty
IQ	–	Intelligence	–	Intellectual capacity
Father self-employed	–	Father entrepreneur	–	–
Other family background	–	Family background	–	–
Age	Knowledge of the world	Leadership	Leadership	–
Education	–	Education	–	–
Self-employment experience	Knowledge of business	–	–	–
Industry experience	–	Knowledge of the trade	–	–
Experience in occupation	Knowledge of occupation	–	–	–
Unemployed at start	Less alternative opportunity for social distinction	–	–	–
Own capital	(reputation to obtain) capital	Own capital	–	Ability to obtain capital
Start motivated by 'challenge'	–	–	More ambition	Willingness important
Self-esteem	–	–	–	Self-confidence

Note: *Cantillon and Kirzner are omitted (to arrange the table conveniently) due to their small contribution to empirically testable determinants of entrepreneurship. Cantilllon stresses only the importance of risk bearing whereas Kirzner's contribution in this respect is limited to emphasizing the role of leadership.

research subjects on the one hand, and to suggest subjects that are worthwhile considering for future empirical research on the other. Real progress in entrepreneurship research can be achieved today (with current methods and databases) by empirically testing yesterday's views.

Notes

*   *De Economist*, **147**(3), 1999, 311–35, 'Some classic views on entrepreneurship', C.M. van Praag, © 1999. Reprinted with kind permission of Springer Science and Business Media.

1.   Hébert and Link (1988) provide the most famous historical overview of entrepreneurship. Their objective is different from mine, which is reflected in their approach. They aim at giving a complete overview of the history of economic thought of entrepreneurship. They therefore link historical theories as put forth over time to each other. My diverging objective and approach are defined below.

2.   He infused the term with precise economic content. Imprecise usage of the term 'entreprendeur' existed prior to Cantillon.

3.   'Et que tout le Troc [Trade] et la circulation de l'Etat se conduit par l'entremise de ces Entrepreneurs' (Cantillon [1755] 1979, p. 73).

4.   'Un Entrepreneur qui promet de paier au Propriétaire, pour sa Ferme ou Terre, une somme fixe d'argent, sans avoir de certitude de l'avantage qu'il tirera de cette entreprise' (ibid., p. 59).

5.   'La variation journaliére de prix . . . rend leur profit incertain' (ibid., p. 61). And a few pages further: 'tout cela cause tant d'incertitude parmi tous ces Entrepreneurs, qu'on en voit qui font journallement banqueroute' (p. 63).

6.   Cantillon made his own fortune as a banker in Paris (Hébert and Link, 1988, p. 15).

7.   'Il faut que quelques-uns qui seront les plus mal achalandés fassent banqueroute' (Cantillon [1755] 1979, p. 65).

8.   As of 1978, some neoclassical formalized models have been built in which the entrepreneur's role has been resurrected.

9.   See Barreto (1989).

10. These 'new combinations' include the introduction of a new good or service, a new method of production, the opening of a new market, the conquest of a new source of supply of raw materials or the implementation of a new organization.

11. The concept 'entrepreneur' is broader than the conventional concept in the sense that an entrepreneur should not necessarily direct his own business in order to be an entrepreneur, but narrower in the sense that not every independent business director is an entrepreneur.

12. In *The Theory of Economic Development* ([1911] 1934), Schumpeter sees the formation of a new firm as the most typical case of a new combination. However, in his book *Business Cycles* (1939, pp. 94–6) large monopolistic firms that block potential competition carry out most innovations (compare Heertje, 1993, pp. 44–52).

13. Schumpeter admits that other economists would object. Equilibrium conditions imply quantifying equations that do not allow for psychic magnitudes.

14. That is, the (real) uncertainty pertaining to any business venture.

15. The need for ability to forecast varies with production sectors, depending on the length of the production process and on the variability of wants: the more basic the wants the producer aims to satisfy, the more stable and predictable they are.

PART II

ENTREPRENEURSHIP SELECTION/VENTURE START-UPS

3 Willingness and opportunity to start up as an entrepreneur

> The law of 'survival of the fittest' states that those organisms tend to survive which are best fitted to utilize the environment for their own purposes. Those that utilize the environment most, often turn out to be those that benefit those around them most; but sometimes they are injurious. Conversely, the struggle for survival may fail to bring into existence organisms that would be highly beneficial. (Marshall [1890] 1930, p. 242)

Introduction

Governments are by and large of the opinion that new firm formation is necessary for a healthy economy and that 'natural' entrepreneurship supply is insufficient. As a result, governments started to provide encouragement programmes for self-employment, and studies to evaluate their effectiveness became desirable. The objective of self-employment encouragement programmes is to stimulate potential successful entrepreneurs to switch to this occupational status, or to provide enthusiastic would-be entrepreneurs with an opportunity to become entrepreneur. In order to recruit programme participants efficiently, these categories of would-be entrepreneurs should be located. This calls for insight into the individual decision process.

In this chapter, I shall distinguish between opportunity and willingness to become an entrepreneur. Individuals only become entrepreneurs when they are willing *and* have the opportunity to do so. This chapter aims at identifying individual determinants of both opportunity and willingness. Observing someone as being an entrepreneur implies that the individual has both been willing and had the opportunity to switch to this occupational status. If either *willingness* (motivation) or *opportunity* (ability and/or capital) is absent, the individual will not start up as an entrepreneur. I shall define the unobserved concepts opportunity and willingness in such a way that both their levels should surpass specific threshold levels for somebody becoming an entrepreneur: opportunity and willingness are each necessary conditions and together they are sufficient for entrepreneurship.

I shall identify the contribution of these unobservable variables, that is, opportunity and willingness, to the entrepreneurship decision by estimating a specific model that can cope with the special requirements that: (i) opportunity and willingness are unobserved concepts; (ii) only if they both surpass a certain threshold level do we observe an individual as an entrepreneur, and (iii) individuals fail to become entrepreneurs whenever they have an insufficient level of willingness, of opportunity, or of both. Such a model is called a bivariate probit model with partial observability and was first used by Dale Poirier in 1980. I shall employ it in order to answer the following questions empirically: do individuals who do not become an entrepreneur lack opportunity, willingness or both, and what are the observable variables that explain the underlying unobserved concepts 'opportunity' and 'willingness' to become self-employed? I shall answer these questions by means of a dynamic approach, that is, by analysing the probability of *becoming* rather than the probability of *being* an entrepreneur.

In both theoretical and empirical studies various definitions of 'entrepreneur' are used (see Chapter 1). I do not presume to add a definition of my own, but I do need an operational definition. The empirical observed phenomenon that is used here (and has been used in most empirical research) is self-employment. Individuals who report being self-employed and those who are sole owners of their incorporated businesses are counted as entrepreneurs.

This chapter is organized as follows. The next section defines opportunity and willingness to become an entrepreneur and explains why I distinguish between them. I relate the model and its determinants to a long tradition in the economics of entrepreneurship, going back to Say (1803); Marshall (1890); Schumpeter (1911); and Knight (1921) (see Chapter 2). The third section explains Poirier's bivariate probit model, which is used to distinguish the unobservable phenomena of opportunity and willingness. The fourth section describes the data used for this study (the US National Longitudinal Survey of Youth) and the variables used. The model is estimated from a subsample of white male labour force participants (between 20 and 31 years old) who were not self-employed in any year from 1985 to 1988 and who were either (un)employed or self-employed in the next year (1986–89). I focus on white male labour force participants for reasons of homogeneity and for comparability with other studies. The survey, selected because it contains appropriate information on a large number of observations, imposes the restriction on age. Its panel character makes it possible to focus on the dynamics of starting up as an entrepreneur. The fifth section discusses the estimates of the empirical model. The results show that lack of opportunity debars more people from self-employment than insufficient willingness. Opportunity in turn is dependent on the availability of capital (assets and real estate). These capital requirements can be compensated by a low regional unemployment rate and by entrepreneurship experience. The results are in accordance with the views of Say and Knight. The final section concludes and summarizes the main findings.

Opportunity and willingness

I define opportunity as the possibility of becoming an entrepreneur if one wants to. Important variables determining opportunity are start-up capital, entrepreneurial ability and the (macro)economic environment. Individuals who are willing to start up as an entrepreneur have an opportunity to do so whenever they possess enough capital, or can borrow it. It is likely that loans are dependent on the perceived (entrepreneurial) ability of the would-be entrepreneur, given economic conditions. This implies that ability and capital resources are substitutes: the opportunity to start up as an entrepreneur increases with a (weighted) sum of both.

Willingness to start up as an entrepreneur is defined as the valuation of work in self-employment versus remaining (un)employed, in otherwise identical situations. Willingness is positive whenever entrepreneurship is seen as the best available (career) option. Consequently, willingness is dependent on both individual preferences for the special features of entrepreneurship as well as the alternative available options and their perceived attractiveness.

My wish to distinguish entrepreneurial willingness from opportunity within a dynamic framework is based on my own intuition and on my reading of the classical literature (see Chapter 2). In contrast to recent contributions, the distinction between opportunity and willingness is quite prominent in this literature. Say ([1803] 1971) stresses the importance of the availability of a scarce combination of certain moral qualities (ability) necessary for being an entrepreneur. Capital may be borrowed, but only by people who have some additional qualities:

> It is commonly requisite for the entrepreneur himself to provide the necessary funds. Not that he must be already rich, for he may work upon borrowed capital; but he must at least be solvent, and have the reputation of intelligence, prudence, probity and regularity. . . . These requisites shut out a great many competitors. (Ibid., p. 330)

Marshall's view ([1890] 1930) largely agrees with Say's. They both argue that ability (though defined differently) is a restricting factor for the supply of individual entrepreneurship. Marshall's entrepreneur can borrow capital, though surviving is easier for hose who supply their own capital. Schumpeter ([1911] 1934) argues that ability does not play a significant role, while capital can be borrowed easily. For Schumpeter, the prime restriction on the supply of entrepreneurs is a scarce combination of motivating forces (willingness) of pursuing indirect instead of direct consumption (see Chapter 2).

Knight (1921 [1971]) argues that capital, due to moral hazard (see LeRoy and Singell, 1987), and willingness, unlike ability, are necessary to start as an entrepreneur: 'Willingness plus power to give guarantees, not backed up by ability, will evidently lead to a dissipation of resources, while ability without the other two factors will be merely wasted' (Knight [1921] 1971, p. 283).

The empirical estimates will identify the relative importance of opportunity (ability and capital) and willingness and the estimates will thereby show which of the (classical) views is sustained by these findings.

This study aims at contributing to the literature in three ways. The first is the identification of the separate contributions of opportunity and willingness in the decision process to become an entrepreneur. The survey material used by Blanchflower and Oswald (1998) indicates that there are more people who would like to become self-employed than the actual number of self-employed. Their analysis based on satisfaction data points at serious impediments to entrepreneurship. I shall supply an additional instrument to verify whether opportunity rather than willingness forms the bottleneck in this process.

The only 'serious impediment' that Blanchflower and Oswald isolate is the liquidity or capital constraint. Moreover, Evans and Jovanovic (1989), Evans and Leighton (1989), de Wit (1993), Holtz-Eakin et al. (1994b), Lindh and Ohlsson (1996), Blanchflower and Oswald (1998) and Dunn and Holtz-Eakin (2000) all find evidence that capital constraints bind, each using different approaches. The second feature of this model is that it may uncover whether there are other impediments to entrepreneurship opportunity, keeping motivation or preferences for switching to self-employment constant. This will answer the question: is it possible to compensate for a lack of capital by, for instance, entrepreneurial ability?

A third contribution is to evaluate what observable variables affect the probability of switching through the opportunity and willingness components of the decision to become an entrepreneur. For example, suppose we observe (in a univariate framework) that married men are more inclined to become self-employed than single men. Is this then due to the superior willingness of married men (on average), the greater number of opportunities available to them (on average), or perhaps that they are less willing but face far more opportunities? One does not know, unless a differentiation is made between opportunity and willingness in an estimable model. Differentiating between these two concepts also helps us to evaluate whether certain observable individual characteristics affect willingness and opportunity in an opposite sense.

Model

The concepts of willingness and opportunity are not observed. I only observe whether an individual becomes self-employed. I know that, by definition, men who choose to become self-employed have more willingness and more opportunity than the threshold levels (normalized to zero). I also know that men who choose not to start up as an entrepreneur have less than zero willingness or less than zero opportunity or both. I need an empirical model that uses the available information (revealed preferences) as an input and is able to identify the unobserved underlying concepts. Poirier (1980) discusses a joint-decision model that meets these requirements. It is known as the bivariate probit model with partial observability.[1]

Define two individual specific latent variables, I_{1i}^* representing opportunity and I_{2i}^* willingness, where i distinguishes individuals. A linear relation links these constructs to observed individual characteristics, represented by the vector $\mathbf{Z}$.

$$I_{1i}^* = \mathbf{Z}_{1i}\gamma_1 - \varepsilon_{1i} \tag{3.1}$$

$$I_{2i}^* = \mathbf{Z}_{2i}\gamma_2 - \varepsilon_{2i,} \tag{3.2}$$

where $\mathbf{Z}_{ji}$ ($j = 1,2$) is the vector of potential influential individual characteristics, γ_j, is a vector of unknown parameters that will measure the effect of $\mathbf{Z}$ on I_{ji}^* and ε_{ji} is an error term with mean 0 and (normalized) variance 1. I assume that the error terms have a bivariate standard normal distribution with correlation ρ and are independent from one observation to another. Define two (still unobserved) dummy variables:

$$I_{ji} = 1 \text{ if } I_{ji}^* > 0 \quad \text{and} \quad I_{ji} = 0 \text{ otherwise.} \tag{3.3}$$

Hence, I_{1i} equals one for an individual with (sufficient) opportunity to become self-employed and zero for a man without (sufficient) opportunity. I_{2i} equals one if and only if an individual is (sufficiently) willing to become self-employed and is zero otherwise. I observe whether an individual becomes self-employed (that is, the realization of the dichotomous variable $I_i = I_{1i}^* I_{2i}$). Consequently, the probability of switching to entrepreneurship equals:

$$Pr(I_i = 1) = Pr(I_{1i}^* > 0, I_{2i}^* > 0) = Pr(\varepsilon_{1i} < Z_{1i}\gamma_1, \varepsilon_{2i} < Z_{2i}\gamma_2)$$
$$= F(Z_{1i}\gamma_1, Z_{2i}\gamma_2, \rho), \tag{3.4}$$

where $F(.,.,.)$ is the standard normal cumulative distribution function. Maximum likelihood estimates of the parameters in this model, that is, γ_1, γ_2 and ρ can be obtained by maximizing the log-likelihood function:

$$\log L = \sum_{i=1}^{N} \left\{ I_i \log[F(Z_{1i}\gamma_1, Z_{2i}\gamma_2, \rho)] + (1 - I_i)\log[1 - F(Z_{1i}\gamma_1, Z_{2i}\gamma_2, \rho)] \right\},$$

$$\tag{3.5}$$

where N is the number of observations. The estimation of this function will result in the identification of the significant determinants of both opportunity and willingness and will furthermore lead to an evaluation of the relative importance of both opportunity and willingness for the start-up probability of an individual.[2]

Data: construction and choice of variables

The empirical model is estimated on a sample drawn from the US National Longitudinal Survey of Youth (NLSY79).[3] The first interview among the approximately 12000 respondents was held in 1979 when they were between 14 and 22 years old. Since then, these extensive interviews have been repeated annually. The most recent year at my disposal for this study is 1989. For reasons of homogeneity, I use a subsample of 3790 white males.

The observed dependent variable, which I call 'switch', takes on the value 1 in year t if a white male labour force participant, who was not self-employed in year t, reports being self-employed in year $t+1$.[4] It takes on the value 0 for labour force participants (excluding the self-employed) in year t who have not become self-employed in year $t+1$.[5] The observable variable 'switch' summarizes for each young man whether the required amounts of opportunity and willingness are present in a given year. Table 3.1 shows that switches are rather rare.[6]

Therefore, I am forced to pool observations from the last five years. I proceeded as follows: the frequency of observation is annual. I assume that a switch between year t and year $t+1$ is best explained by the values of the variables in year t. I selected all individuals for whom switch = 1 in 1985, 1986, 1987 or 1988. The values for year t were assigned to the explanatory variables of these switchers, with dependent variable 1. Of the 24 individuals who switched more than once, I randomly retained one year of

Table 3.1   Self-employment and switches in the NLSY79

Year	Labour force	Self-employed	Switches
$N = 3790$			
1985	3488	171	71
1986	3561	196	77
1987	3597	208	96
1988	3630	231	74
1989	3643	246	
Total			318

observation and deleted the other.[7] This left me with 294 (318–24), observations for whom switch = 1. For the remaining observations (individuals for whom switch = 0 during all periods under study), four sets of regressor values (1985, 1986, 1987 and 1988) are available. I have randomly assigned one of these four sets to each of these individuals. Individuals in the resulting sample, consisting of 3451 labour force participants who are not currently self-employed, are between 20 and 31 years old. I created a 'year dummy' variable that denotes the year of observation to check whether time effects occur. The procedure yields a switch percentage of 100%*(294/3451) = 8.5 per cent. The origins of the pooled data are summarized in Table 3.2.

Apart from the time-dependent explanatory variables there is time-independent information such as parental background variables, formal education and so on. I also constructed some longitudinal variables, such as experience in self-employment. The variables that I use in the final analysis are defined in Table 3A.1 in the appendix. After deleting observations with missing values for at least one variable, 2244 out of 3451 observations remained. Table 3A.2 shows the descriptive statistics for this subsample.

Besides the differences between the groups of switchers and non-switchers, there is another interesting set of differences: between switchers before and after their switch. These differences are shown in Table 3.3.

Switchers stem from a variety of industrial and occupational origins, though especially from the construction and trade (wholesale and retail) industries and the occupation 'craftsman'. Furthermore, 45 per cent of the switchers remain within their own industry, 45 per cent within their occupation and 28 per cent within one industry and one occupation. On average, these (self-selected) individuals gain both in satisfaction and in rate of pay as they switch; but their mortgages increase considerably.

Table 3.2   Origins of pooled data

Year	Not self-employed labour force participants including switchers	Switches
1985	842	59
1986	872	75
1987	884	92
1988	853	68
Total	3451	294

Table 3.3   Switchers before and after the switch

Variable	Before	After
Industry (%)		
Agriculture	5.7	9.4
Construction	25.9	34.0
Manufacturing	13.8	6.7
Transportation/communication	2.7	5.1
Trade	22.6	12.5
Business and repair	8.8	15.5
Professional services	7.7	5.7
Others	12.8	11.1
Occupation (%)		
Professional/technical	9.1	11.1
Managers	9.4	14.8
Craftsmen, foremen	34.7	40.7
Operatives	12.5	9.4
Farmers	2.6	2.5
Sales	6.7	4.7
Service workers	7.7	4.7
Others	17.3	12.1
Job satisfaction (1–4)	3.3	3.6
Average hourly rate of pay ($)	8.6	11.6
Standard deviation of rate of pay ($)	4.9	8.6
Mortgage loan ($)	4500	65 100

To identify my empirical model, and indeed to identify opportunity and willingness, I have to impose at least one exclusion restriction. I make two assumptions:

1. The opportunity equation is dependent on the variable 'self-employment experience measured in years' and the willingness equation on the dummy variable 'ever been self-employed'. This seems a sensible assumption to make: the ability to borrow money ('opportunity') is likely to depend upon previous experience as an entrepreneur. The relation between willingness and previous length of self-employment experience is less obvious, although the mere fact that a person has been self-employed is likely to have an impact on willingness.

2. Following Knight ([1921] 1971) and more recent empirical research, I expect wealthier people to have a higher propensity to become

self-employed. I assume capital to affect this propensity exclusively through opportunity and not through willingness.[8]

I want to stress that the identification of 'opportunity' and 'willingness' depends critically upon these exclusion restrictions.[9]

With respect to the explanatory variables, some of the following comments relate a variable directly to 'opportunity' or 'willingness', but note that I initially use every variable in both the 'opportunity' and the 'willingness' equations. The explanatory variables mentioned in assumptions 1 and 2 above are exceptions.

Psychological variables

Social psychologists strongly believe that a measure of internality of an individual's locus-of-control beliefs is a determinant of successful entrepreneurship. The Rotter scale (Rotter, 1966) is such a measure. The lower an individual's Rotter scale, the less internal are his locus-of-control beliefs and the more he perceives the outcome of an event as beyond his personal control. The dichotomous Rotter-scale measure derived from the NLSY79 is equal to 1 for more 'internal' individuals.

Moreover, social psychologists (see Hornaday and Aboud, 1971) have found a low religious value among entrepreneurs. I include a dummy for people who adhere to stricter religions (Lutheran and Methodist) to verify whether they are less willing to become self-employed. Furthermore, the descriptive statistics suggest including a dummy that differentiates men who have been extremely outgoing (extroverted) children from the more introverted ones.

Human capital variables

Human capital variables, such as age, education, or experience in self-employment are supposed to explain both opportunity and willingness to switch to self-employment. These kinds of variables are included in the opportunity equation because human capital is supposed to affect the entrepreneurial abilities (perceived by the lender). Inclusion of human capital variables in the willingness equation is justified by their expected effect on the availability and desirability of alternative labour market options. Education, self-employment experience, the respondent's age and the frequency of former job changes are included in the (final) willingness equation.

Situational variables

Other variables can directly influence a potential lender's decision (perhaps because they affect entrepreneurial ability) and also one's willingness to start up as an entrepreneur: whether a person is currently unemployed, whether he works in the public sector (instead of the private sector), whether he has severe health limitations and whether he is married. The population density of the area in which an individual lives might have an impact on both opportunity and willingness. An indicator for this is the dummy variable 'central city' that is one for individuals living in densely populated areas and zero otherwise.[10]

Moreover, the macroeconomic environment may directly affect the opportunity for an individual to become self-employed. An indicator for this is the regional (and temporal) unemployment rate, included in the NLSY79.

Table 3A.3 contains the results of the saturated model in which all explanatory variables listed above, except for the ones relating to the assumptions, were part of both equations. On the basis of this model I chose the specification presented in the next section.[11]

Estimation results and inferences
Table 3.4 summarizes the final estimation results. I shall comment on the key results reflected in this table.

Financial variables
The estimated assets coefficient does not diverge from the recent empirical findings by Evans and Jovanovic (1989 and others mentioned earlier in this chapter): a lack of assets restrains the opportunity to become self-employed. But the effect is relatively small once the dummy for real estate ownership is added. This variable gives scope to the possibility that the additional security that real estate owners can offer to potential lenders (in case of future bankruptcy) influences individual business formation opportunity. Black et al. (1996) find in their more macro-oriented study that the supply of collateral affects business formation in the UK significantly. Table 3.3 showed that young men who switch to self-employment indeed increase their mortgage loans considerably. Table 3.4 shows that ownership of collateral affects individual (perceived) business opportunities to a large extent.

Psychological variables
The Rotter scale, measuring respondents' internal-locus-of-control beliefs, has no significant effect: either on opportunity or on willingness. Evans and Leighton (1989) also found no significant effect of being 'internal' on the transition probability. It was possible that this insignificance was due to unidentified opposing forces of internality on opportunity and willingness. However, the related variable 'outgoing as a child', which has not previously been implemented in this type of study, has a highly significant and

Table 3.4   Estimation results: bivariate probit[1]

Variable	Opportunity equation			Willingness equation		
	Coefficient	(*t*-value)[2]	Derivative[3]	Coefficient	(*t*-value)[2]	Derivative[3]
Financial variables						
Assets	0.006	(1.72)*	0.001			
Real estate	0.825	(2.91)***	0.125			
Psychological variables						
Rotter	−0.352	(1.70)*	−0.053	0.467	(1.48)	0.028
Lutheran/ Methodist				−0.277	(1.79)*	−0.017
Outgoing child	−0.335	(1.40)	−0.051	1.217	(2.11)**	0.073
Human capital variables						
Age	−1.686	(2.04)**	−0.255	1.741	(2.12)**	0.105
Age squared/10	0.354	(2.12)**	0.054	−0.374	(2.34)**	−0.022
Education	−0.014	(0.40)	−0.002	−0.031	(0.63)	−0.002
Self-empl. expr.	0.353	(2.18)**	0.053			
Dummy self-expr.				0.574	(1.17)	0.034
Job changes				0.054	(3.26)***	0.003
Situational variables						
Unemployed	0.116	(0.27)	0.017	−0.374	(0.64)	−0.022
Public sector	−0.503	(1.79)*	−0.076	0.632	(1.37)	0.038
Married	0.177	(0.76)	0.027	−0.526	(1.72)*	−0.032
Handicap	0.223	(1.10)	0.034			
Low unempl. rate	0.731	(2.12)**	0.110			
Central city	−0.329	(1.29)	−0.050	0.998	(2.30)**	0.060
Constant	19.653	(1.91)*	2.970	−19.664	(1.88)*	−1.181
Rho	−0.757	(3.33)**				
Log likelihood	−692					
Number of cases	2244					

Notes:
1. The estimates are obtained in Gauss. I verified the results using Limdep. Differences are negligible.
2. The reported absolute *t*-values are based on White's heteroscedastic consistent estimate of the covariance matrix. Coefficients are significant at the 1% level if the corresponding absolute *t*-value is at least 2.58 (marked with ***), at the 5% level if the corresponding absolute *t*-value is at least 1.96 (marked with **). They are marginally significant (at the 10% level) if the corresponding *t*-value is at least 1.65 (marked with *).
3. Because the coefficients in such a non-linear model are difficult to interpret, derivatives are shown in the third column. These derivatives give the effect of a unit change of the independent variable for the average individual in the sample on the probability that is explained.

positive effect on willingness to switch. Men who were outgoing as children are significantly more willing to become self-employed.

The negative coefficient of the religion dummy variable in the willingness equation (taking on value one for the two strict religions, that is, Lutheran or Methodist) renders some weak empirical support for a low entrepreneurial interest among believers.

Variables related to self-esteem are omitted because they lacked any significance, unlike Say's predictions ([1803] 1971, pp. 241–3).

Human capital variables
The data show that 24 year olds have the worst opportunities to start a business. On the other hand 23 year olds are the most willing to do so of all ages. Most of the young men in the sample are older than 24. Therefore, opportunity is an increasing function of age and willingness a decreasing function of age for most individuals in the sample. The findings with respect to age are consistent both with Evans and Jovanovic's (1989) presumptions and with Miller's (1984) occupational choice model.

Education does not affect the probability of becoming self-employed, either through willingness, or through opportunity. Self-employment experience is a significant determinant of opportunity.[12] For the average young male in the sample, one additional year of experience in self-employment increases the probability of having the opportunity to become self-employed again by a significant 5.3 per cent.[13] Say ([1803] 1971) has already pointed at the importance of 'knowledge of business' for successful entrepreneurship. An alternative explanation for this positive effect is unobserved heterogeneity. However, this alternative explanation is not sustained by a significant influence of former self-employment experience on willingness. The dummy for self-employment experience included in the willingness equation shows that the fact that one has been self-employed in the past does not affect the motivation to become self-employed again. On the one hand, individuals may have become very enthusiastic, even though they quit; on the other, they may have become disillusioned.

The frequency of former job changes has a positive effect on the willingness to become self-employed. This is consistent both with a positive approach, that is, entrepreneur types change jobs frequently because they like changes (as in Schumpeter [1911] 1934) and with the negative approach that frequent job changers are associated with displaced persons (as in Shapero, 1975; Evans and Jovanovic, 1989).

Situational variables
Unemployed young white males in the United States do not have fewer opportunities and are not more willing to become self-employed in

comparison with their (privately) employed counterparts.[14] Public sector workers have somewhat less opportunity to switch to self-employment than employees in the private sector. This result is corroborated by the finding that 71 per cent of the founders of the fastest growing US companies got their entrepreneurial idea, which is part of the opportunity, through previous employment (Bhide, 1994). This source of ideas is generally not available to public sector workers. Public sector workers are not significantly less willing to make the transition.

I predicted that married men would have more opportunity to become self-employed than bachelors, as husbands have wives who either save personnel costs or supply the family with a fixed income. Moreover, I presumed married men to be less willing to engage in a (risky) entrepreneurial venture due to their family responsibilities. The empirical evidence renders only marginal support for the second presumption.

A low (regional and temporal) unemployment rate, defined as a rate lower than 3 per cent, raises the opportunity to start a business significantly: some 11 per cent for the average sampled individual. The effect of living in a central city (instead of in a less densely populated area) is not significant on opportunity and positive on willingness. Whether an individual is physically disabled does not seem to influence his opportunities to start a business.

By means of alternative specifications of the opportunity and willingness equations, I found some additional results: the interview year that corresponds to each individual selected in the sample is not significant in explaining opportunity and willingness. Parental background (measured by the father's and mother's education levels, the father's occupation and language usage at home) does not add anything to the explanation either. Also, Brockhaus's finding (1980) that extremely unsatisfied wage workers are pushed into self-employment is not sustained by the data: low reported job satisfaction did not affect willingness to become an entrepreneur.

Table 3.4 demonstrates ρ to be negative and significant. Apparently the error terms of the willingness and opportunity equations are correlated. Consequently, the model differs significantly from the nested bivariate probit model with partial observability: the sequential case, see note 8.

Figure 3.1 shows what kind of distribution within the willingness and opportunity region the estimates generate. Apparently, there are far more individuals willing to become self-employed than individuals who have an opportunity. The number of entrepreneurial starts would be almost seven times as high if everyone who wishes to start had the opportunity to do so. This finding is consistent with research results by Blanchflower and Oswald (1998): there are more individuals who wish to switch to self-employment than the actual number of switchers. This result is also consistent with

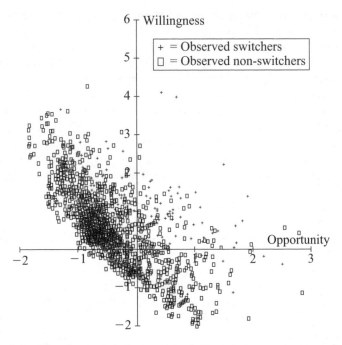

Figure 3.1   Distribution of observations by imputed opportunity and willingness

the several stories about capital restrictions and higher satisfaction among the self-employed (Blanchflower and Oswald, 1998). Table 3.5 shows what percentage of individuals, self-employed and employed in reality, belongs to each of the quadrants in Figure 3.1.

In order to compare this study with others, I have also estimated a univariate ('regular') probit model with identical independent variables. This model simply estimates the determinants of the decision to switch to self-employment. I have calculated what percentage of actual entrepreneurs is accurately predicted to become an entrepreneur, using each of the models. The percentage resulting from the regular approach is 10.6, much lower than the comparable estimate of 28 per cent resulting from the bivariate approach. This is some indicator that the bivariate approach is superior indeed. Univariate probit estimation results are shown in Table 3.6.

The parameter estimates themselves differ from the bivariate approach with respect to a number of variables. The effect of the stricter religions is significant here: adhering to one of the stricter religions renders a significantly lower probability of switching to self-employment. The coefficient of

Table 3.5   Estimated percentages in each of the quadrants in Figure 3.1

Quadrant	Total	Self-employed	Employed
Willingness > 0, opportunity > 0	7.7	28.0	5.0
Willingness ≤ 0, opportunity > 0	12.3	6.4	13.1
Willingness > 0, opportunity ≤ 0	69.0	61.7	69.9
Willingness ≤ 0, opportunity ≤ 0	11.0	3.8	12.0

Table 3.6   Estimation results: univariate probit

Variable	Coefficient	(Absolute t-value)[1]	Derivative[2]
Financial variables			
Assets	0.007	(2.22)**	0.001
Real estate	0.739	(5.99)***	0.128
Psychological variables			
Rotter	−0.075	(0.86)	−0.012
Lutheran/Methodist	−0.202	(1.95)*	−0.035
Outgoing child	0.302	(2.82)***	0.052
Human capital variables			
Age	−0.156	(0.64)	−0.027
Age squared/10	0.028	(0.58)	0.005
Education	−0.037	(2.24)**	−0.006
Self-employment expr.	0.218	(2.99)***	0.037
Dummy self-expr.	0.520	(3.35)***	0.089
Job changes	0.038	(4.29)***	0.006
Situational variables			
Unemployed	−0.124	(0.89)	−0.021
Public sector	−0.107	(0.70)	−0.018
Married	−0.198	(2.44)**	−0.034
Handicap	0.180	(0.90)	0.030
Low unemployment rate	0.755	(2.26)**	0.129
Central city	0.175	(1.62)	0.030
Constant	0.830	(0.27)	0.142
Log likelihood	−708		
Number of cases	2244		

Notes:
1. The reported absolute t-values are based on White's heteroscedastic consistent estimate of the covariance matrix. Coefficients are significant at the 1% level if the corresponding absolute t-value is at least 2.58 (marked with ***), at the 5% level if the corresponding absolute t-value is at least 1.96 (marked with **). They are marginally significant (at the 10% level) if the corresponding t-value is at least 1.65 (marked with *).
2. Because the coefficients in such a non-linear model are difficult to interpret, derivatives are shown in the third column. These derivatives give the effect of a unit change of the independent variable for the average individual in the sample on the probability that is explained.

the bivalent variable that indicates whether one has self-employment experience has become significant, besides the effect of self-employment experience measured in years. More highly educated young men have a significantly lower probability of switching to entrepreneurship. The coefficient for the bivalent dummy variable that indicates whether a young man is married is significantly negative. This is consistent with the findings by both Evans and Jovanovic (1989) and Evans and Leighton (1989).

The decomposition of (opportunity and willingness) effects is not easily derived from this aggregate approach by inspection: some surprises remain. This was also the case in the application of Abowd and Farber (1982). Meant as an instrument to decompose regressor effects on the propensity to start up as an entrepreneur into effects on opportunity and willingness, the bivariate approach is also a valid instrument for finding significant effects that are hidden as insignificant effects in the aggregate.

Inferences

What can we infer from these estimation results? To investigate this, I compare the simulated probability of becoming self-employed of a reference individual with the probability of an individual who deviates from the reference one with respect to one variable only. The reference individual is defined as having average values for continuous variables and the modal outcome for categorical variables.

Table 3.7 shows the differences in probability due to changes in one of the independent variables in each category. This difference is large (and significant) if the reference individual suddenly becomes an owner of real estate: this renders a probability difference of almost 23 per cent. A reference individual who faces a capital increase of one standard deviation, $\sigma = \$11\,250$, experiences a probability increase of 2.7 per cent only. Both self-employment experience (measured in years) and a low regional unemployment rate (dummy variable) can compensate for a lack of assets and real estate: they both strongly increase the probability of becoming self-employed by 31 and 19 per cent, respectively.

Conclusions

Individuals who start up as entrepreneurs have not only perceived enough opportunity to do so, but they have also perceived this career option as the most attractive one. In other words, they have the opportunity and willingness to become self-employed. Individuals who do not switch to self-employment are not willing or do not have the opportunity or both. This chapter separates the unobserved concepts of opportunity and willingness for young white male Americans. I assumed that opportunity and willingness are explained by a (partly distinct) set of observed explanatory

Table 3.7   Simulated probabilities of becoming self-employed

	Pr(switch)	Difference with reference individual	($|t$-value$|$)
Reference individual	0.075		
Financial variables			
Real estate	0.302	0.227	(3.62)***
Assets $+ \sigma$	0.102	0.027	(1.65)*
Assets $- \sigma$	0.071	-0.004	(1.83)*
Psychological variables			
Outgoing as a child	0.097	0.022	(0.81)
Human capital variables			
Self-employment expr. $+ \sigma$	0.387	0.312	(3.00)***
Situational variables			
Low unemployment rate	0.269	0.194	(1.08)

Note: The reported absolute *t*-values are based on White's heteroscedastic consistent estimate of the covariance matrix. Coefficients are significant at the 1% level if the corresponding absolute *t*-value is at least 2.58 (marked with ***). They are marginally significant (at the 10% level) if the corresponding *t*-value is at least 1.65 (marked with *).

variables. Opportunity includes variables that are observed equivalents for both capital and entrepreneurial ability, given economic conditions. It is argued that the opportunity to start up as an entrepreneur is positively present for men having sufficient assets. If not, capital lenders should be convinced that the potential lender has enough entrepreneurial ability. Whereas opportunity and willingness are both necessary conditions (and together sufficient) to become an entrepreneur, capital and ability are assumed to be potential substitutes for meeting the necessary opportunity condition.

A bivariate model with partial observability is estimated on a subsample of the NLSY79. The annual data are pooled in a particular way to obtain a sufficient number of observed switches. The resulting sample includes 264 switches. The key empirical results are:

- The overwhelming majority of young men in the United States are willing to become self-employed. If the opportunity is given to anyone, the realized number of switchers would multiply by seven. Opportunity evidently forms the bottleneck in the individual decision process.
- Opportunity is largely determined by capital requirements. These in turn are primarily dependent on real estate ownership. The opportunity for entrepreneurship is also affected by the regional

unemployment rate and by entrepreneurial ability, mainly through self-employment experience and age.
- Willingness is positively affected by outgoingness, by the number of job changes and by whether one lives in a central city or in a less densely populated area. More mature men (above 23) are less willing to become self-employed. Religious and married people have a lower probability of being willing to become self-employed, though not very significantly so. Other variables are insignificant.
- Entrepreneurial ability serves to a certain extent as a substitute for capital requirements. The kind of entrepreneurial ability that increases the opportunity to start largely coincides with entrepreneurial experience.
- As capital seems to be a necessary requirement for becoming self-employed (for starters without experience in entrepreneurship) and since willingness is no constraining factor, I conclude that the US evidence supports Knight's ideas. A first start in entrepreneurship requires assets or collateral. This finding, pointing at binding capital constraints, is in accordance with other empirical estimates by Evans and Jovanovic (1989), among others. However, the additional finding that experience in entrepreneurship results in a perceived entrepreneurial ability that can serve as a substitute for own capital or real estate is in accordance with the related ideas of Say. Schumpeter's vision is empirically not supported: motivational factors appear not to be the prime constraints in the individual supply of entrepreneurship.

In Part III (Chapter 6) I shall investigate the individual determinants of lasting and successful entrepreneurship for the subsample of individuals who have shown to be willing and in a position to start up as an entrepreneur. This gives scope to a comparison of the determinants of opportunity and willingness on the one hand, and those of performance on the other. Such a comparison will lead, as we shall see in Chapter 9, to valuable policy recommendations. First, however, I shall focus on the role that risk attitude plays for the decision to start up as an entrepreneur. It has already become apparent from the discussion of the classic contributions to the determinants of successful entrepreneurship that risk attitude is a debated determinant of entrepreneurship.

Appendix 3A

Table 3A.1   Definition of the variables selected

Variable	Definition
Switch	Dependent variable: = 1 if respondent switches from wage employment to self-employment
Assets	Total amount of assets (in $1000)
Real estate	Dummy: = 1 if respondent owns some real estate
Rotter	Dummy: = 1 if respondent feels 'direction of life is in control'
Lutheran or Methodist	Dummy: = 1 if respondent's religion is Lutheran or Methodist
Outgoing child	Dummy: = 1 if respondent reports having been an extremely outgoing child
Age	Respondent's age (in years)
Education	Number of years of formal education
Labour experience	Years of total labour market experience
Dummy self-empl. expr.	Dummy: = 1 if respondent has self-employment experience
Job changes	Reported number of different jobs ever had
Unemployed	Dummy: = 1 if respondent is unemployed
Public sector	Dummy: = 1 if respondent is public sector worker
Married	Dummy: = 1 if respondent is married
Handicap	Dummy: = 1 if respondent has health limitations
Low unemploym. rate	Dummy: = 1 if regional unemployment rate is less than 3%
Central city	Dummy: = 1 if respondent lives in a central city

Table 3A.2   Descriptive statistics

Variable	Switchers		Non-switchers		All	
	Mean	(s.d.)	Mean	(s.d.)	Mean	(s.d.)
Observations	264		1980		2244	
Switch					0.118	(0.32)
Assets	6.240	(25.33)	3.200	(7.60)	3.560	(11.28)
Real estate	0.190	(0.39)	0.051	(0.22)	0.066	(0.25)
Rotter	0.750	(0.44)	0.770	(0.42)	0.760	(0.42)
Lutheran or Methodist	0.140	(0.34)	0.190	(0.39)	0.180	(0.39)
Outgoing child	0.170	(0.38)	0.100	(0.30)	0.110	(0.31)
Age	25.460	(2.65)	25.320	(2.61)	25.340	(2.62)

Table 3A.2   (Continued)

Variable	Switchers		Non-switchers		All	
	Mean	(s.d.)	Mean	(s.d.)	Mean	(s.d.)
Education	12.590	(2.46)	12.790	(2.45)	12.770	(2.45)
Self-empl. expr.	0.610	(1.16)	0.120	(0.49)	0.170	(0.63)
Dummy self-expr.	0.320	(0.47)	0.080	(0.27)	0.110	(0.31)
Job changes	8.240	(4.87)	6.690	(3.88)	6.870	(4.03)
Unemployed	0.072	(0.26)	0.084	(0.28)	0.082	(0.28)
Public sector	0.053	(0.22)	0.085	(0.28)	0.081	(0.27)
Married	0.370	(0.48)	0.440	(0.50)	0.430	(0.50)
Handicap	0.038	(0.19)	0.029	(0.17)	0.030	(0.17)
Low unempl. rate	0.019	(0.14)	0.006	(0.08)	0.008	(0.09)
Central city	0.160	(0.37)	0.110	(0.31)	0.120	(0.32)

Table 3A.3   Estimation results of the saturated model: bivariate probit[1]

Variable	Opportunity equation			Willingness equation		
	Coefficient	(t-value)[2]	Derivative[3]	Coefficient	(t-value)[2]	Derivative[3]
Financial variables						
Assets	0.007	(1.68)	0.000			
Real estate	0.864	(2.85)	0.123			
Psychological variables						
Rotter	−0.374	(1.17)	−0.053	0.526	(1.08)	0.029
Lutheran/Methodist	−0.053	(0.66)	−0.007	−0.228	(0.25)	−0.013
Outgoing child	0.031	(0.33)	−0.044	1.328	(1.46)	0.073
Human capital variables						
Age	−1.605	(1.60)	−0.228	1.780	(1.81)	0.098
Age squared/10	0.340	(1.66)	0.048	−0.382	(1.92)	−0.021
Education	−0.023	(0.36)	−0.003	−0.024	(0.30)	−0.001
Labour experience	−0.022	(0.26)	−0.003	−0.010	(0.08)	−0.000
Self-empl. expr.	0.362	(1.82)	0.051			
Dummy self-expr.				0.635	(0.95)	0.035
Job changes	0.011	(0.02)	0.002	0.045	(1.44)	0.002
Situational variables						
Unemployed	0.178	(0.57)	0.025	−0.056	(0.65)	−0.031
Public sector	−0.435	(1.21)	−0.062	0.547	(0.98)	0.030
Married	0.139	(0.45)	0.020	−0.509	(0.80)	−0.028
Handicap	0.091	(0.12)	0.013	0.200	(0.18)	0.011
Low unempl. rate	0.316	(0.39)	0.045	0.777	(0.40)	0.043
Central city	−0.302	(1.08)	−0.043	1.032	(1.72)	0.057

Table 3A.3 (*Continued*)

Variable	Opportunity equation			Willingness equation		
	Coefficient	$(t\text{-value})^2$	Derivative^3	Coefficient	$(t\text{-value})^2$	Derivative^3
Constant	18.647	(1.49)	2.648	−20.116	(1.54)	−1.108
Rho	−0.679	(1.88)				
Log likelihood	−691					
Number of cases	2244					

Notes:
1. The estimates are obtained in Gauss. I verified the results using Limdep. Differences are negligible.
2. The reported absolute t-values are based on White's heteroscedastic consistent estimate of the covariance matrix. Coefficients are significant (at the 5% level) if the corresponding absolute t-value is at least 1.96. They are marginally significant (at the 10% level) if the corresponding t-value is at least 1.65.
3. Because the coefficients in such a non-linear model are difficult to interpret, derivatives are shown in the third column. These derivatives give the effect of a unit change of the independent variable for the average individual in the sample on the probability that is explained.

Notes

1. I do not know of any other empirical application of this model. Maddala (1983), who describes this model extensively, does not mention an empirical application either.
2. Poirier (1980) has shown that γ_1, γ_2 and ρ are identified as long as Z_{1i} and Z_{2i} do not contain exactly the same variables and the explanatory variables exhibit sufficient variation. The exogenous variables must take on at least as many distinct data configurations as there are unknown parameters in the model, indicating that if a model contains a number of variables taking on many different values, no identification problems will occur (see ibid., p. 215).
3. The NLSY79 is a publicly available panel data set that is designed and maintained by the US Department of Labor, Bureau of Labor Statistics. It is part of a set of surveys, called the NLS. The National Longitudinal Surveys (NLS) set of surveys are designed to gather information at multiple points in time on the labour market activities and other significant life events of several groups of men and women. For more than 3 decades, NLS data have served as an important tool for economists, sociologists, and other researchers.
4. Individuals who start incorporated businesses are included.
5. Switch is probably an underestimate of the real fraction of starters, because self-employment spells that started but ended between interviews are not counted.
6. The reason why Table 3.1 starts in 1985 will be given below.
7. The way a 'switch' is defined renders a maximum of two switches per individual. The number of men who switched twice is very small. It hardly makes sense to treat double switches as a separate state. Therefore, I randomly select one of the switches and delete the other in these cases. Due to the correlation of the error terms I cannot treat a double switch as two observations.
8. I disregard the possibility that wealthier people might have lower absolute risk aversion, making them more willing to become self-employed (as in Kanbur, 1979 and Kihlstrom and Laffont, 1979).
9. In principle it is possible to estimate the model only under the first restriction. However, in that case identification becomes very thin. Maddala (1983, p. 279) discusses an

alternative model that deals with multiple decision functions and partial observability. An empirical example of this model can be found in Abowd and Farber (1982). It is nested in Poirier's model, unlike the univariate probit model. Maddala defines Poirier's model as the joint case and the model by Abowd and Farber as the sequential case. In the sequential case I_{2i}^* is a useful concept only for those observations that meet the condition $I_{1i}^*>0$. For instance, consider the question whether a certain individual is matched to a particular job. Suppose the job vacancy is advertised; at the start there are no candidates. In order for the match to be realized the individual should first apply for the job and then be hired by the employer. Individuals who do not apply will certainly not be hired because $I_{1i}^*\leq 0$ and therefore I_{2i}^* can never take on a positive value. 'Nothing ventured, nothing gained'. This sequential case is obtained from the joint case by the parameter restriction $\rho=0$. Further, in this chapter I shall show which one of the two bivariate models with partial observability suits the survey data best.

10. Population densities are based on statistics per Standard Metropolitan Statistical Area (SMSA). These are approximately 150 regions as defined by the US Census Bureau.
11. I imposed six restrictions and performed a likelihood ratio test (test statistic is 2.69). I conclude that the restricted model is not rejected in favour of the saturated model.
12. Self-employment experience is obtained before 1985 (but as of 1979, the first interview year). The 24 men who have switched twice may also have gathered this experience afterwards, depending on whether their first or second switch has been randomly selected.
13. The measurement of this variable is not perfect: I increased self-employment experience by the number of weeks between the current and previous interview divided by 52 whenever somebody reported at both interviews that they were self-employed.
14. We also included 'unemployment experience' in the relationships and found that this does not affect either willingness or opportunity. Surveys on the (ambiguous) relation between unemployment and self-employment can be found in Storey (1991) and Meager (1992).

4 Risk aversion and the choice for entrepreneurship

Introduction

It is common knowledge that the rewards of entrepreneurship are more variable and less certain than the wages of employment. This stylized fact has been based on substantial empirical support (for instance in de Wit, 1993). A logical consequence should be that individuals with a relatively low degree of risk aversion are more likely to opt for entrepreneurship as opposed to wage employment. This view was held by classic authors like Cantillon (1755), Say (1803) and Knight (1921). More recently it has surfaced in models of occupational choice by Kanbur (1979), Kihlstrom and Laffont (1979) and Blanchflower and Oswald (1998). Nevertheless, this widely accepted effect of risk aversion discouraging people from entrepreneurship has never been put to an empirical test. I assume that this omission is mainly due to a lack of sample surveys in which a direct individual measure of risk aversion (and entrepreneurship history) is recorded.[1]

In this chapter I discuss the results from a first attempt to fill this gap by means of a sample survey constructed for this purpose (second section). It contains sufficient information of occupational histories of approximately 1700 individuals along with their evaluations of a specified lottery and other explanatory variables. The answers to the lottery evaluation result in a snapshot proxy of individual attitudes towards risk. From this, we derive from utility theory an empirical measure of both absolute risk aversion as well as relative risk aversion (third section). These empirical measures are subsequently inserted into (probit) regression equations explaining self-employment selection, which is the conventional empirical equivalent of entrepreneurship (see Chapters 2 and 3). I control for several important other potential determinants of self-employment (fourth section). The results suggest that risk aversion discourages people from entrepreneurship. However, the causality of this finding is far from clear-cut. More research into empirical measures of risk attitude is clearly needed.

Data

The data set is unusual and deserves some attention.[2] In 1952, a survey was conducted among 5800 children in the last grade of elementary school in the Dutch province of Noord-Brabant, recording their ability, school performance, family background and related variables. Thirty years later, these records were rediscovered, and from a search of local population registers 4700 of the original respondents could be traced. A questionnaire was sent to all of them, requesting information about education, household composition, labour market status and earnings. After two reminders, interviewers approached the remaining male non-respondents. (For financial reasons only men were interviewed, as their labour force participation rate is higher; this explains the small proportion of women in the sample.) The response rate among the 4700 individuals located was 58 per cent (2700 individuals).

The same sample was interviewed (by post) for a third time in 1993. This time our objective was to complete labour market histories and in particular to gather information about entrepreneurship experiences. The intersecting sample that provides individual records for 1953, 1983 and 1993 contains almost 2100 individuals who have ever participated in the labour force.

The resulting data set has some distinct features. First, all individuals were born in 1939 or 1940, so the sample is homogeneous with respect to age and epoch. Second, all individuals were living in the same region, Noord-Brabant, at the age of 12. But a comparison with national statistics shows that the sample is nevertheless representative of the Netherlands: many variables relating to labour force participation, industrial structure and earnings are the same as in the country as a whole. Another interesting feature is the availability of early childhood variables, such as scholastic ability and intelligence at a young age.

Three variables deserve a more detailed description for the present purpose:

- *Entrepreneurship*   Dependent variable, dummy which takes on the value 1 for individuals who have ever been self-employed, and 0 for all other respondents who have ever been part of the labour force.
- *Risk attitude*   The last interview in 1993 includes the question how much the respondent would pay for a ticket in a hypothetical lottery with ten tickets and a single prize of 1000 guilders.[3] This reservation price $\bar{p}$ reflects the individual attitude towards risk. A drawback of this measure of risk aversion is its *ex post* character.
- *Wealth*   A monetary measure of an individual's net assets in the last interview year, recorded as a class variable, in ten classes. Item non-response is high; my estimate of the quality of the answers given is low. Moreover, it is difficult to believe that a measure of *ex post* wealth affects occupational choice (if any, the effect would be the other way around). For these reasons, I consider utility functions that

presume constant relative risk aversion, as these should make use of the wealth measure, with great caution.

The inclusion of the other (control) variables in the model is motivated by the existing theoretical and empirical knowledge base of entrepreneurship. Note that I cannot include any time-varying variables, since past labour market decisions are being explained. Those individuals who have never become entrepreneurs have not taken this decision in a particular year. This explains why variables such as age are not included among the explanatory variables. Moreover, there is another category of variables defined only for entrepreneurs: this applies, for instance, to motivation to start up as an entrepreneur, industry dummies, macroeconomic circumstances in the starting year or specific experience in the industry and/or occupation selected for entrepreneurship. These too are omitted from the analyses.

The model is estimated on a subsample of approximately 1700 individuals who have ever participated in the labour market and for whom the relevant variables are not missing.

Measures of risk aversion
In the present context, the reservation price $\tilde{p}$ is the price respondents would pay for a ticket in a hypothetical lottery with ten tickets and a single prize of 1000 guilders. My approach is to use transformations of it as variables influencing the choice between wage employment and entrepreneurship in a probit analysis. The novelty of this treatment (if any) lies in the use of a *direct* measure of risk aversion rather than an *ex post* revealed attitude.

The simplest way to use the reservation price $\tilde{p}$ as a measure of risk aversion is to consider a simple transformation of the reservation price,

$$\tilde{\tilde{p}} = 1 - \frac{\tilde{p}}{100},$$ (4.1)

where 100 is the fair value of the lottery ticket in guilders. A more sophisticated approach is to use the Arrow–Pratt measure of absolute risk aversion:

$$\rho = \frac{-U''}{U'},$$ (4.2)

where U is a common utility function $U(W)$ of wealth or rewards W. The role of ρ can be demonstrated in a simple framework. Consider two alternatives X and Y. X offers a *certain* reward X, and Y gives additional benefits B with probability α or irretrievable costs C with probability $1 - \alpha$. The choice between these two options depends on the sign of an indicator function:

$$I = E(U_Y) - U(X) + K, \qquad (4.3)$$

where the constant K allows for individual characteristics and for other aspects of X and Y than mere rewards. In standard expected utility theory,

$$E(U_Y) = \alpha U(X + B) + (1 - \alpha)U(X - C). \qquad (4.4)$$

I approximate both terms by a Taylor series:

$$U(X + B) = U(X) + BU'(X) + \tfrac{1}{2}B^2 U''(X)$$

$$U(X - C) = U(X) - CU'(X) + \tfrac{1}{2}C^2 U''(X).$$

Substituting these approximations into (4.4) leads to the following expression for the operative term of (4.3):

$$E(U_Y) - U(X) = [\alpha B - (1 - \alpha)C]U'(X) + \tfrac{1}{2}[\alpha B^2 + (1 - \alpha)C^2]U''(X). \qquad (4.5)$$

I first apply this expression to the choice between paid employment X (supposedly free from risk) and entrepreneurship Y at equal expected rewards. This condition implies $\alpha B - (1 - \alpha)C = 0$ so that (4.5) is simplified to:

$$E(U_Y) - U(X) = \tfrac{1}{2}dB^2 U''(X),$$

with d equal to the odds ratio $d = \alpha/1 - \alpha$. After dividing by $U'(X)$ (which is always positive) this can be rewritten as:

$$\frac{E(U_Y) - U(X)}{U'(X)} = \tfrac{1}{2}dB^2\rho, \qquad (4.6)$$

with ρ the absolute risk aversion of (4.2). It follows at once that, at equal expected rewards, the uncertain alternative Y is the more attractive the lower is the absolute risk aversion.

The same framework can be applied to participation in a lottery as the uncertain option Y. If α is the probability of winning a single prize Z and the price of a ticket is p, the benefit B equals $Z - p$ and the cost C is p.

Since purely pecuniary considerations prevail, K of (4.3) is zero, and participation depends on the sign of (4.5), or:

$$E(U_Y) - U(X) = [\alpha(Z - p) - (1 - \alpha)p]U'(X)$$
$$+ \tfrac{1}{2}[\alpha(Z - p)^2 + (1 - \alpha)p^2]U''(X).$$

The *reservation* price $\tilde{p}$ of an individual will make this expression zero. This gives:

$$(\alpha z - \tilde{p})U'(X) = -\tfrac{1}{2}(\alpha Z^2 - 2\alpha Z\tilde{p} + \tilde{p}^2)U''(X),$$

so that:

$$\text{absolute } \rho = \frac{-U''}{U'} = \frac{\alpha Z - \tilde{p}}{\tfrac{1}{2}(\alpha Z^2 - 2\alpha Z\tilde{p} + \tilde{p}^2)}, \qquad (4.7)$$

and this permits the calculation of the individual absolute risk aversion from the answer to the lottery question. It is of course questionable whether the absolute or the relative risk aversion is constant and permanent (as is assumed in the empirical analysis). We therefore introduce relative risk aversion as the third risk measure,

$$\text{relative } \rho = \text{absolute } \rho * \textit{wealth}, \qquad (4.8)$$

where *wealth* is the respondent's wealth as recorded in the 1993 survey, at the same time as the reservation price. But this has been measured crudely, by a single question, the replies being classified in a few wide classes. Nevertheless, in the next section I shall show the results from using all three measures of risk aversion, that is, as given by (4.1), (4.7) and (4.8).

Results

The three measures of risk aversion are based on the observations presented in the Appendix Table 4A.1. The table shows that reservation prices above ten guilders cluster at multiples of five. In Table 4.1, I have compressed this information in standard intervals of risk attitude. The data clearly suggest that entrepreneurs are less risk averse than employees.

In Table 4.2, each of the three risk variables is introduced in a standard probit analysis of retrospective occupational choice. The respondents have replied to the lottery question and have been employed or self-employed (or both) at any time in their adult life; if they report self-employment at any time, as 15 per cent do, this signifies a choice for entrepreneurship. Apart from risk attitude and wealth, five background variables from the

Table 4.1   Descriptive statistics

Variable	Employees		Entrepreneurs	
	Mean	*(s.d.)*	*Mean*	*(s.d.)*
Reservation price	23.94	(34.99)	32.91	(49.26)
Absolute ρ	$1.56*10^{-3}$	$(0.67*10^{-3})$	$1.38*10^{-3}$	$(0.88*10^{-3})$
	Number	*Percentage*	*Number*	*Percentage*
Risk averse	1352	89.2	249	80.3
Risk neutral	142	9.4	53	17.1
Risk loving	21	1.4	8	2.6

1952 interview have been included after a prolonged search for relevant covariates. Reported wealth is wealth, summarily recorded in the 1993 survey and listed in broad classes, with several observations negative and many zero; there is probably severe under-reporting, and the low sample mean will affect relative ρ and contribute to the low quasi-elasticity. As for the background variables, intelligence is an intelligence quotient with special reference to abstract reasoning, measured while at school in 1952. Gender has value 1 if female. Vocational schooling is 1 if the highest level of education attended, as reported in 1993, is MBO (Middelbaar Beroeps Onderwijs), a vocational type of schooling, often business oriented, its level somewhat below college. Father independent is 1 if the respondent's father was self-employed; and the dummy variable 'father high education' is 1 if he has a university education. Both variables were recorded in 1952.

For continuous independent variables, I report quasi-elasticities, that is, the effect of a 1 per cent change on the probability of entrepreneurship, expressed in percentage points; for bivalent (0,1) dummy variables derivatives give their direct effect in percentage points. All coefficients have been evaluated at the sample mean, and absolute *t*-values are given in brackets. The top of the table refers to the three risk measures and wealth, all from the 1993 survey, which I discuss presently; the second half lists five background variables. These are gender, intelligence, educational level and two parental characteristics. None of the other available variables proved significantly relevant. Further details are given in the notes to the table.

The major finding is that all three measures of risk aversion have a clear negative effect on entrepreneurship. The relative ρ is tainted by its association with reported wealth, which is poorly measured: *ex post* wealth is by itself quite strongly positively related to entrepreneurship, and as a result relative ρ has a positive coefficient unless we control for reported wealth. The introduction of this variable then affects the fit as well as the coefficients

Table 4.2 *Probit analysis of entrepreneurship*

Variable	Coef.	$(t)^2$	Coef.	$(t)^2$	Coef.	$(t)^2$	Coef.	$(t)^2$
					Quasi-elasticities			
Transformed price (4.2)			−0.11	(3.0)***				
Absolute ρ (4.7)					−0.13	(3.1)***		
Relative ρ (4.8)							−0.04	(2.3)**
Reported wealth							0.18	(9.2)***
Intelligence	0.38	(2.4)**	0.37	(2.2)**	0.37	(2.2)**	0.21	(1.2)
					Derivatives			
Gender	−0.27	(5.7)***	−0.26	(5.2)***	−0.25	(5.3)***	−0.22	(4.4)***
Vocational schooling	0.14	(2.5)**	0.15	(2.6)***	0.15	(2.6)***	0.13	(2.1)**
Father independent	0.28	(6.3)***	0.28	(6.2)***	0.28	(6.2)***	0.20	(4.1)***
Father high education	0.28	(2.4)**	0.28	(2.4)**	0.28	(2.4)**	0.12	(1.0)
Number of observations[1]	1787		1787		1787		1699	
Log likelihood	−0.402		−0.400		−0.399		−0.360	

Notes:
1. The number of observations in the last column is smaller because of non-response in the wealth question. The other analyses are not materially altered if repeated on the smaller subset of data.
2. The reported absolute *t*-values are based on White's heteroscedastic consistent estimate of the covariance matrix. Coefficients are significant at the 1% level if the corresponding absolute *t*-value is at least 2.58 (marked with ***), at the 5% level if the corresponding absolute *t*-value is at least 1.96 (marked with **).

of the background variables, which are otherwise immune to the introduction of risk. But reported wealth is a 1993 variable, and jointly endogenous with the individuals' work experience. It has very little to do with *initial* wealth, which may well affect the entrepreneurship decision, and there is no point in including it in the other analyses where it is not needed as a control variable.

Conclusion

Entrepreneurship is indeed discouraged by the individual degree of risk aversion. The evidence is consistent with the historical theoretical contributions by Cantillon, Say, Marshall, Knight and Kirzner, but in contradiction to the other theoretical contribution discussed in Chapter 2, that is, by Schumpeter. The evidence is also consistent with some (relatively) more recent influential theoretical contributions, like these by Kanbur (1979) and Kihlstrom and Laffont (1979). This conclusion is inevitably subject to serious reservations. The analysis perforce uses a mixture of variables recorded in 1952 and in 1993 in an attempt to explain the individual's entrepreneurship choices in the intervening years. The three risk-aversion measures are from 1993, and it is tacitly assumed that they describe an individual trait that is constant over life. This would seem to hold more readily for absolute ρ than for relative ρ. But if risk aversion by whatsoever definition is reduced by the experience of entrepreneurship or by income or wealth, this would certainly alter the interpretation of the results. The biggest problem with the current approach is probably the timing of the information. I have an indication of risk aversion only (long) after the occupational choice has been made, and I am not able to deal adequately with the problem of variation in risk attitude over the individual's lifetime with the present data.

Appendix 4A

Table 4A.1   Frequency distribution of reservation prices

Reservation price	Employees	Entrepreneurs
Non-response	52	20
0	184	55
1	115	20
2	43	8
3	13	0
5	108	15
7	1	0
10	472	80

Table 4A.1 (Continued)

Reservation price	Employees	Entrepreneurs
12	2	0
15	10	1
20	10	0
25	294	49
50	92	21
60	1	0
75	5	0
80	1	0
99	1	0
100	142	53
110	6	0
120	1	0
125	2	2
150	4	1
200	5	4
250	2	0
500	1	1
Total	1567	330

Notes

1. One other study pertaining to Finland, which has been carried out a few years later, reports comparable results with the study that I discuss in this chapter (see Ekelund et al., 2000).
2. The analyses in Chapter 5 are based on the same sample. This also motivates my rather extensive description here.
3. Its value was about $500 at that time.

PART III

ENTREPRENEURSHIP SUCCESS/VENTURE PERFORMANCE

5 Entrepreneurship selection and labour demand

> There is a far more close correspondence between the ability of businessmen and the size of the businesses they own than at first sight would appear probable. (Marshall [1890] 1930, p. 312)

Introduction

In conditions of persistent high unemployment it is important to increase the demand for labour, and one way of doing so is to encourage the creation of new firms that hire employees. As Kaldor stated in 1934 in his seminal article 'The equilibrium of the firm', the determinant production factor for the size of any (mature) firm is the coordinating ability of the entrepreneur leading the firm. There can be at most one coordinator, coordinating all transactions in which the firm is involved, thereby restricting the size of the firm. The amount of all other factors of production employed is limited by the fixed supply of coordinating ability by the unique entrepreneur. In another seminal contribution, Coase (1937) argued similarly: that there are 'diminishing returns to management' in the sense of decreasing returns to scale at a given level of entrepreneurial ability.

Therefore, talented persons should be particularly induced to become an entrepreneur, for these will be most successful in creating labour demand. Knowledge of the determinants of the choice for entrepreneurship and of successful entrepreneurship may help to develop policies to this end.

In this chapter I develop an integrated model that considers the individual decision to become an entrepreneur as well as the ensuing firm size. Individuals who become an entrepreneur start a new business or purchase an existing business (as in Holmes and Schmitz, 1995). Whether a member of the labour force becomes an entrepreneur or an employee depends on the associated utilities. These in turn depend on ability and on individual risk attitude, since entrepreneurship is a risky business (see also the evidence obtained in the previous chapter). In the present analysis, as in Chapter 4, relative risk aversion is an observed attribute of the individual. Entrepreneurial talent determines the size of the business. This talent is a function of observable characteristics.

The model owes much to the recent literature, starting with Lucas (1978), as will be shown in the second section; but various views of the entrepreneur as decision maker, combiner of resources, risk taker or manager are of course much older and provide (again) a suitable backdrop to the present analysis (see Chapter 2). These classic contributors laid the foundations on which this model is built. The view of the entrepreneur as independent owner, decision maker, combiner of resources and manager of the firm has been adopted by Say, Marshall and Knight. All authors (with the notable exception of Schumpeter) stress that entrepreneurs moreover bear all uncertainty or risk, in contrast to employees.

The interpretation of risk in the current application, that is, as due to an individual's ignorance of his own abilities until they have been revealed in action, comes closest to the views of Marshall and Knight, who acknowledged that entrepreneurial ability should be backed up by good luck. As became clear in Chapter 2, all classic theorists assume that potential profit, as compared to wages, is the major incentive to become an entrepreneur; and so it is in this model.

The third section describes the model and the fourth, the data. In the fifth section I discuss the results of estimating the model on the sample of Dutch labour force participants that was also employed for the analysis in Chapter 4. The final section 6 summarizes and concludes.

Links with recent literature
In equilibrium models with full employment of a given labour force some people become entrepreneurs and found firms that employ the others. The actual division between entrepreneurs and wage labour turns on the distribution of individual characteristics among the population. A number of such models have been developed since Lucas's (1978) seminal paper. I follow Lucas in assuming a closed economy with a given workforce that is homogeneous with respect to employee productivity. Each member of the workforce is also endowed with a specific entrepreneurial talent that varies across individuals. The workforce is first divided into entrepreneurs and employees, and the available resources are then allocated among entrepreneurs: a firm consists of the entrepreneur together with the production factors under his control. For Lucas these production factors are a given labour supply and a given quantity of homogeneous capital. However, here I must perforce assume a perfectly elastic capital supply, for the available data give no information about capital ownership and/or investment at the time of inception of the business. The entrepreneur is merely organizing the workforce.

I extend Lucas's model in one important dimension. When choosing occupations, individuals are not certain of their entrepreneurial talent: they choose the occupation that renders the highest *expected* utility, where utility is an Arrow–Pratt transformation of returns by relative risk aversion, which varies between individuals. The model in this respect resembles

Kanbur's (1979) model. This is a model of occupational choice under risk between two occupations: wage earner or employee, in which case a single unit of homogeneous labour is supplied and the risk-free competitive wage is received; or entrepreneur, in which case the individual employs labour and produces homogeneous output according to a production function that includes the individual's entrepreneurial ability. Entrepreneurship is risky since agents do not know their own ability in advance.

In Kanbur's model, individuals apply the common (population) distribution of aptitude, and *perceived* expected ability does not vary among individuals. Here, in contrast, individual expectations of entrepreneurial talent depend on specific personal characteristics. Individuals know the corresponding population distribution of (entrepreneurial) talent, but not the outcome. The actual entrepreneurial talent is an unobserved latent variable. Risk aversion, on the other hand, has been observed in the present data.

Kihlstrom and Laffont (1979) put forward a model in which individuals face the same choice between a risky entrepreneurial career and a riskless wage. They state:

> There are, of course, many factors that should influence this choice. The most important ones would include entrepreneurial ability, labour skills, attitudes toward risk, and initial access to the capital required to create a firm. The present paper focuses on risk aversion as the determinant which explains who becomes an entrepreneur and who works as a labourer. (Ibid., p. 720)

Hence, all these models, developed in the late 1970s, describe the division of a given workforce over the two classes of entrepreneurs and employees, or employers and employees. This division depends on the distribution of individual characteristics. For Lucas (1978) this is entrepreneurial aptitude, in addition to capital; for Kanbur (1979) and for Kihlstrom and Laffont (1979) the emphasis is on risk attitude with respect to entrepreneurial aptitude, which remains unknown until it has been proved.[1]

In this application, we treat both risk aversion and ability as major determinants. We attempt an empirical analysis with entrepreneurial ability as a latent variable and with risk aversion observed (after a fashion) in a structural econometric model of equilibrium. This calls for several unrealistic short cuts (one wage level, a homogeneous workforce of employees and so on) that will become apparent as I proceed. I shall therefore compare the estimation results of this 'restricted' structural model approach to reduced-form results: this gives some indication about the robustness of the model estimates.

The model
We establish the importance of risk attitude and entrepreneurial ability by an empirical analysis of the labour market experience of Dutch individuals,

who have been interviewed three times at intervals of 30 and 11 years. It is known from these interviews whether the individual has ever been an entrepreneur, and if so how many people his firm has employed. I also have an indication of his risk attitude (see Chapter 4). Moreover, the interviews provide a number of background variables at a younger age. Apart from size, little is known about the firm. This is reflected by the model specification.

The model allows for both perceived ability and risk attitude as determinants of the choice for entrepreneurship. Success, as measured by the size of the firm's workforce, depends on actual ability. For ease of exposition we distinguish two decisions:[2]

1. The first choice for an individual is to start as a full-time entrepreneur or to work as a full-time employee. Individuals know their own risk attitude, R_i, and their person-specific *distribution* of entrepreneurial talent θ_i. However, the precise value of entrepreneurial talent remains unknown until it is put to the test. Consequently, individuals base their first decision on known risk attitude and the relevant distribution of entrepreneurial talents.
2. The individual's actual entrepreneurial talent θ_i is revealed in practice to those who start up as an entrepreneur. At the equilibrium value of the unique wage rate, entrepreneurs decide how many wage workers to employ. This second decision determines L_i, the total workforce of each firm, including the entrepreneur. Its minimum is 1, and I assume that this value holds whenever the optimal workforce is smaller, given that the firm exists.

Distributions and specifications adopted
The individual's perception of entrepreneurial ability θ_i is distributed log normally:

$$\log \theta_i = \mathbf{X}_i \beta + \varepsilon_i, \tag{5.1}$$

where $\mathbf{X}_i$ is a vector of individual characteristics such as education, gender and family background. The parameter vector β will be estimated. Entrepreneurial ability is supposed to be stochastic due to, among other factors, a yet unknown level of good luck.

As in Kanbur's model, the operation of the economy is governed by the production function: $F(L, \theta_i) = \theta_i L^\gamma$, where γ is the parameter which measures the output elasticity of labour and lies between 0 and 1. With a single input, γ also indicates the returns to scale of the production process; these are assumed to be decreasing.[3]

The utility function is $U_i = (y_i^{1-R_i})/(1 - R_i)$, which implies that $R_i = [-U_i''(y)y]/[U_i'(y)] \cdot R_i$ is the Arrow–Pratt measure of relative risk aversion, $R \neq 1$ (compare to ρ as given by (4.8) in Chapter 4). A negative R_i indicates that i is a risk lover, a zero R_i that i is risk neutral and a positive R_i that i is risk averse. Income y is either entrepreneurial profit π or the unique wage rate w. Profits are uncertain because they depend on the unknown amount of entrepreneurial ability of the individual.

A brief guide to the solution of the model
Individuals assess the potential values of labour demand and profit for the occupational choice question. Knowledge of the levels of potential labour demand, profit and the wage rate, in addition to the basic knowledge that individuals have (about the distribution of θ_i, the level of R_i, and the production and utility functions), is a sufficient basis for a proper occupational choice.

After the working population has split up into entrepreneurs and employees and an estimate of the wage rate has been formed, each entrepreneur selects the profit-maximizing size of his firm, that is, the working force L_i, which includes the entrepreneur in addition to his employees. If the realized value of θ_i turns out to be low once the decision in favour of entrepreneurship has been made, a firm of unit size will have been started, and in such a firm the profit level can be suboptimal.[4]

In the exposition below, a circumflex indicates potential values.

Solution step 1: calculating potential gains of entrepreneurship All individuals consider the potential gains of entrepreneurship that they can realize. Potential profit is $\hat{\pi}_i = \theta_i \hat{L}_i^\gamma - w\hat{L}_i$. Output prices are normalized to unity and labour is the only scarce input, priced w. Hence, the profit-maximizing workforce is:

$$\hat{L}_i = \left(\frac{\gamma\theta_i}{w}\right)^{1/(1-\gamma)} \tag{5.2}$$

at a profit:

$$\hat{\pi}_i = \left(\frac{\gamma\theta_i}{w}\right)^{1/(1-\gamma)}\left(\frac{1-\gamma}{\gamma}\right)w.$$

Since θ_i is random, so are $\hat{L}_i$ and $\hat{\pi}_i$. Solving the above system yields log $\hat{L}_i$ and log $\hat{\pi}_i$ as linear functions of θ_i so that they have log-normal distributions, too. The means and variances are for log $\hat{L}_i$:[5]

$$\frac{x_i^{\mathrm{T}}\beta}{1-\gamma} + \frac{1}{1-\gamma}\log\left(\frac{\gamma}{w}\right), \frac{\sigma^2}{(1-\gamma)^2}; \tag{5.3}$$

and for log $\hat{\pi}_i$:

$$\frac{x_i^T \beta}{1-\gamma} + \frac{\gamma}{1-\gamma} \log\left(\frac{\gamma}{w}\right) + \log(1-\gamma), \frac{\sigma^2}{(1-\gamma)^2}.$$

The utility of an entrepreneur has a log-normal distribution:

$$\log U_i^e \sim N(a, b^2), \tag{5.4}$$

where:

$$a = \frac{1-R_i}{1-\gamma} X_i \beta + \frac{1-R_i}{1-\gamma} \gamma \log\left(\frac{\gamma}{w}\right) + (1-R_i)\log(1-\gamma)$$

$$- \log(1-R_i); \, b^2 = \left(\frac{1-R_i}{1-\gamma}\right)^2 \sigma^2.$$

The utility associated with wage employment is:

$$\log U_i^w = (1-R_i)\log w - \log(1-R_i). \tag{5.5}$$

Solution step 2: choosing occupations   The entrepreneurship decision is modelled as a discrete choice, based on the (expected) utility of the alternatives. The individual is indifferent between entrepreneurship and wage employment when the utility of w and the *expected* utility of $\hat{\pi}_i$ are equal, with the expectation taken over the log-normal distribution.[6] The condition for the equality of $U(w)$ and $E[U(\hat{\pi}_i)]$ (or of their logarithms) can be derived from the earlier equations, and it can be expressed in a threshold value or reservation demand for labour. Between individuals, differences in their characteristics x_i and their risk attitude R_i determine who becomes an entrepreneur and who does not; these observed variables enter into the condition that Elog $\hat{L}_i$ (which depends on x_i) exceeds the threshold set by labour reservation demand log c_i, which can be derived as:[7]

$$\log c_i = \frac{\sigma^2}{2(1-\gamma)^2}(R_i - 1) + \log \gamma - \log(1-\gamma). \tag{5.6}$$

In the empirical analysis I use Elog $\hat{L}_i > \log c_i$ as the condition for entrepreneurship.

Solution step 3: determining firm sizes   The labour force has split up in a group of entrepreneurs and a group of employees. Employees earn w and entrepreneurs employ L_i individuals including themselves. L_i and π_i depend on the realized value of θ_i:

$$\log L_i = \frac{\log \theta_i}{1 - \gamma} + \frac{1}{1 - \gamma} \log\left(\frac{\gamma}{w}\right) \tag{5.7}$$

$$\log \pi_i = \frac{\log \theta_i}{1 - \gamma} + \log(1 - \gamma) + \frac{\gamma}{1 - \gamma} \log\left(\frac{\gamma}{w}\right). \tag{5.8}$$

If the realized value of θ_i turns out to be less than w/γ, then, according to (5.7), $L_i < 1$ but the entrepreneur should operate with the suboptimal amount of labour $L_i = 1$.

Solution step 4: determination of the wage level   In equilibrium w is such that total labour demand is equal to given aggregate labour supply of N persons,

$$\sum_{i \in I} L_i \equiv N, \tag{5.9}$$

where I is the group of entrepreneurs, its size endogenously determined. Substituting the expected value of L_i in the left-hand side, we find:[8]

$$\log w = (1 - \gamma)\log\left[\frac{\sum_{i \in I} \exp\left(\frac{x_i^T \beta}{1 - \gamma}\right)}{N}\right] + \log \gamma + \frac{\sigma^2}{2(1 - \gamma)} \tag{5.10}$$

for the wage level and:

$$\log L_i = \frac{\log \theta_i}{(1 - \gamma)} - \log\left[\frac{\sum_{i \in I} \exp\left(\frac{x_i^T \beta}{1 - \gamma}\right)}{N}\right] - \frac{\sigma^2}{2(1 - \gamma)^2} \tag{5.11}$$

for individual labour demand (see Appendix 5A).

The model leaves little room for more realistic assumptions. There is a single wage for all employees, regardless of the hours worked and of talents and expertise.[9] Part-time employment (and part-time entrepreneurship) must be ignored since it is incompatible with the entrepreneurship decisions as an individual discrete choice. Moreover, the model does not allow for employment by public authorities or large corporations that do not owe their existence to the talents of a single individual. The solution in the empirical analysis is to restrict labour supply N effectively to persons who either are (or have been) entrepreneurs or are employed in firms with fewer than 100 employees. During the period under review about 7 per cent of the Dutch labour force was in public service, and over 30 per cent in firms with more than 100 employees.

Finally, there is the apparent conflict between the optimal labour demand derived from marginal conditions and the discrete nature of the firm's workforce. In (5.9) this discontinuity is ignored, and the summation must include some entrepreneurs with an optimal L_i below 1.[10]

Solution step 5: quantifying the underestimate of L *and* w   All entrepreneurs for whom $\theta_i = w/\gamma$ and

$$x_i\beta \geq \log w - \gamma\log\gamma - (1 - \gamma)\log(1 - \gamma) - \frac{(1 - R_i)\sigma^2}{2(1 - \gamma)}$$

operate at a suboptimal level of $L_i = 1$, and a term $1 - (\gamma\theta_i/w)^{1/(1-\gamma)}$ should be added to the left-hand side of (5.9). If these terms sum to K, (5.9) must be amended to refer to a labour supply of $N - K$, not N, and log w from (5.10) differs from the correct value: in lieu of (N, w), we should have used $(N - K, w^*)$, where $w^* > w$. The effect on log w is:

$$(\log w - \log w^*) \sim -(1 - \gamma)[\log N - \log(N - K)]. \tag{5.12}$$

Approximate upper bounds follow from Table 5.1: 55, or 3 per cent of the entrepreneurs have firm size $L = 1$, and this is the maximum K. As the estimate of γ is 0.6, the discrepancy of the wage rate is at most 1.2 per cent; we ignore this in what follows.

Data

The data set employed, the 'Brabant survey' initially refers to 5800 school-children,[11] who were interviewed and tested in 1952, all at the age of 12 and in the last grade of elementary school in the Dutch province, Noord-Brabant. In so far as they could be traced, they were subsequently re-interviewed in 1983 and 1993. The early data cover a rich set of aptitude scores and parental background variables. The later interviews record labour market histories, including detailed information on entrepreneurship experiences.

For present purposes I use a subsample of 1763 individuals: 258 of them answered 'yes' to the 1993 question 'have you ever been self-employed in a firm that you started or purchased?', and 1505 of the remaining sample

Table 5.1   Frequency distribution of reported firm sizes

Size	Number	Percentage
1	55	21
2	32	12
3	34	13
4	23	9
5–6	19	7
7–8	21	8
9–11	18	7
12–16	17	7
17–25	13	5
26–41	15	6
42–71	6	2
72 and over	5	2
Total	258	

reported having been employed by firms with fewer than 100 employees, at any time in their life.

Dependent variables
These are:

1. A dummy variable that is 1 for individuals who have ever been an entre-preneur and 0 otherwise; the entrepreneurs may have started a new firm, but they may also have taken over an already existing firm;
2. An integer L_i representing firm size. For employees this is 0, for entre-preneurs, it equals 1 plus the answer to the 1993 question 'What is the highest number of employees you have (ever had) in your business?'. The reason for recording the maximum number of employees one has (ever) had rather than any other measure of size of staff is that this was thought to be the best available reflection of entrepreneurial talent.[12]

The vector of observed regressor variables X_j determines the systematic variation of entrepreneurial ability θ as defined in the theoretical model, and the coefficients β_j reflect their effect; it is these coefficients that are esti-mated in the empirical model that explains actual firm size. Occupational choice is (indirectly) affected by the same explanatory variables X_j, since it is determined by the individual comparing his or her specific expected potential firm size $\hat{L}_i$ – which in turn depends on $x_i^T\beta$ – to the reservation firm size c_i.

From earlier work on the empirical determinants of the choice for and success in entrepreneurship (see Storey, 1994; Blanchflower and Oswald, 1998; see also Chapter 6), four categories of potential explanatory variables that are available in the data set emerge:

1. *Parental background*   Parents' education level, father's job level and type (self-employed or not), parental household composition, and family status (rated by the pupil's schoolteacher in 1952).
2. *IQ score*   Knowledge/comprehension tests concerning school subjects, measured in 1952.
3. *Education*   Level and type of each educational phase, number of phases, whether the pupil graduated.
4. *Risk attitude*   The observed indicator of individual risk attitude R_i is based on the answer to the following question in the 1993 questionnaire: 'A prize of 1000 guilders is awarded to one of ten lottery entrants. What is the maximum amount (of guilders) you would pay to participate as one of the entrants in this lottery?'. The answer indicates the individual reservation price for this lottery ticket: the average is 24 guilders for non-entrepreneurs and 33 guilders for entrepreneurs (see Table 4.1 in the previous chapter). Risk aversion R_i is measured as $1 -$ answer/100, that is, the measure $\tilde{\tilde{p}}$ from (4.1).[13]

A category of income data is missing. Proper information about individual (potential and reservation) wages is missing: occupational choices occur in all years between the 1950s and 1990s, whereas employee wage data are available for 1983 and 1993 only.

Estimation results

Suppose that we, as outsiders, know entrepreneurial ability θ with the same precision as the individual i in the first period of the model, that is, $\log \theta_i = X_i\beta + \varepsilon_i$, where ε is distributed as $\varepsilon \sim N(0,\sigma^2)$ (see 5.1). Entrepreneurial ability is indirectly observed, through the firm's labour demand (see 5.11) as:

$$\frac{x_i\beta}{1-\gamma} - \log\left[\frac{\sum_{i \in I}\exp\left(\frac{x_i\beta}{1-\gamma}\right)}{N}\right] - \frac{\sigma^2}{2(1-\gamma)^2} + u_i,$$

where $u_i = \varepsilon_i/(1-\gamma)$, and therefore $u \sim N[0,\sigma^2/(1-\gamma)^2]$. However, $\log L_i$ is observed for entrepreneurs only, hence if and only if $\log L_i \geq \log c_i$, where:

$$\log c_i = \frac{\sigma^2}{2(1-\gamma)^2}(R_i - 1) + \log\gamma - \log(1-\gamma)$$

as in (5.6).

The probability that observation i does not refer to an entrepreneur is:

$$\Pr(\log L_i < \log c_i)$$

$$= \Phi\left[1 - \frac{X_i\beta}{\sigma} + \frac{1-\gamma}{\sigma}\mu + \frac{\sigma}{2(1-\gamma)}R_i + \frac{1-\gamma}{\sigma}\log\left(\frac{\gamma}{1-\gamma}\right)\right],$$

where Φ is the cumulative normal distribution, and:

$$\mu = \log\left[\frac{\sum_{i\in I}\exp\left(\frac{X_i\beta}{1-\gamma}\right)}{N}\right].$$

This is all the information available about non-entrepreneurs. The information about entrepreneurs, on the other hand, is richer, since their firm size is also known. We obtain a Tobit-like log likelihood:

$$\sum_{i\in I}\log\Phi\left[1 - \frac{X_i\beta}{\sigma} + \frac{1-\gamma}{\sigma}\mu + \frac{\sigma}{2(1-\gamma)}R_i + \frac{1-\gamma}{\sigma}\log\left(\frac{\gamma}{1-\gamma}\right)\right]$$

$$+ \sum_{i\in I}\left\{\log(1-\gamma) - \log\sigma + \log\phi\left[\log L_i - \frac{X_i\beta}{1-\gamma} + \mu + \frac{\sigma^2}{2(1-\gamma)^2}\right]\right\}.$$

This is the log likelihood that will be maximized to obtain estimates of β, γ and σ.[14]

Table 5.2 shows the estimates in so far as they turn out significantly different from zero.[15] The estimates $\hat{\beta}$ show how regressors shift the entrepreneurial talent distribution.

Parental background
We find that entrepreneurial talent is higher if an individual comes from an entrepreneurial family. In particular, individuals whose fathers had managerial responsibilities in their job, turn out to be more successful entrepreneurs. Entrepreneurial talent is reduced if the father is engaged in unskilled work.

Entrepreneurship is seen as a cultural inheritance that is passed on to next generations within families (Curran and Burrows, 1988). The son of an entrepreneur often experiences daily (directly or through conversation) the challenges and difficulties of the tasks of entrepreneurship and

Table 5.2   Estimates of the structural model

Coefficient	Variable	Estimate	($|t$-value$|$)
Effect on log L:			
$\beta_1/(1-\gamma)$	Female	-1.256	(21.22)***
$\beta_2/(1-\gamma)$	IQ at age 12	0.394	(2.61)***
$\beta_3/(1-\gamma)$	Father self-employed	0.262	(3.20)***
$\beta_4/(1-\gamma)$	Father unskilled work	-0.713	(8.40)***
$\beta_5/(1-\gamma)$	Father manager	0.847	(5.05)***
$\beta_6/(1-\gamma)$	Education (1–7)	0.190	(9.98)***
$\beta_7/(1-\gamma)$	General intermediate level	0.819	(9.99)***
$\beta_8/(1-\gamma)$	Vocational intermediate level	1.104	(13.29)***
$\beta_9/(1-\gamma)$	Arts-oriented education	-0.701	(9.14)***
$\beta_{10}/(1-\gamma)$	Science-oriented education	0.107	(1.66)*
Effect on log c:			
$\sigma^2/2(1-\gamma)^2$	Risk attitude	1.529	(13.25)***
$\sigma^2/(1-\gamma)^2$	Variance of log L	3.057	(13.35)***
γ		0.592	25.74
Log likelihood		-1693	

Note: Coefficients are significant at the 1% level if the corresponding absolute t-value is at least 2.58 (marked with ***). They are marginally significant (at the 10% level) if the corresponding t-value is at least 1.65 (marked with *).

management. This may give a great opportunity to learn the specifics of entrepreneurship. Moreover, having family members involved (or previously involved) in small business ownership and management could provide easier access to capital or other necessary assets (office or plant space or even the business itself) for entrepreneurship. It could also lead to free consultancy, access to business networks and a good reputation with (potential) clients in the (business) community. The results confirm, among others, those of Stanworth et al. (1989), Magnac and Robin (1994) and Blanchflower and Oswald (1998).

Human capital: education and intelligence
Education is found to strongly influence successful entrepreneurship. The higher an entrepreneur's educational level, the bigger are the chances of success. And on top of this general effect, education to intermediate levels has an additional positive effect on success, particularly if it is vocational training. These results are found, while IQ is controlled for. Intellectual capacity itself (as measured by IQ score) has a positive influence on entrepreneurial talent.

These findings are confirmed by several studies. Pickles and O'Farrell (1987) find that Irish entrepreneurs are more highly educated than non-entrepreneurs, but that people with the highest levels of education are less likely to start up as an entrepreneur. Storey (1994) shows the result of many empirical studies to be that educational attainment of the entrepreneur is an important positive determinant of the growth of his firm. In Chapter 7, I shall discuss the relationship between education level and entrepreneurial performance more extensively.

Not only does the level of education affect entrepreneurial talent, but the type of education is also influential. Analytical skills, signalled and/or obtained through a science-oriented type of education, seem to enhance entrepreneurial talent somewhat (only marginally significant). The most probable explanation for the negative effect of an arts-oriented type of education is that people who choose this type of education are less interested in an entrepreneurial career.

The strong effect of education is notable. For employees, this effect is often attributed to the use of educational level attained as a screening variable for intelligence (and perhaps for some other characteristics, such as perseverance) by employers when hiring employees. Employers obviously do not screen entrepreneurs, but education is found to be at least equally important for entrepreneurial success (even after controlling for intelligence). I conclude that additional research is desirable to find out whether the 'screening device' applies to entrepreneurs as well, in the sense that the factors that make for educational success also determine success in entrepreneurship, or that education itself is an investment in human capital for entrepreneurs. Chapter 7 will also elaborate on this issue: it will compare the returns to education for entrepreneurs with the returns to education for employees.

Risk attitude
Risk attitude enters into the model via its effect on individual reservation labour demand. The more risk averse individuals are, the higher their reservation labour demand, and the smaller their chance of becoming an entrepreneur. The model did not measure the effect of risk attitude on entrepreneurial achievement. The empirical finding that risk aversion debars people from entrepreneurship is consistent with the main finding of Chapter 4 and with the ideas that have been present for a long time among both academics and practitioners of entrepreneurship, in the disciplines of economics, (small business) management and (social) psychology.

Gender
Women are clearly at a disadvantage in their achievements as entrepreneurs (confirming the results of, for instance, Blanchflower and Oswald, 1998).

The survey refers to a generation of women, born in 1940, who had many problems in entering the labour market (Storey, 1994). These problems may result from their responsibilities at home (commitments to children), which may limit their input (time and effort) in the business, to an extent that it is insufficient for the business to be healthy. Their possible lack of credibility with capital suppliers may mean that they encounter difficulties in obtaining sufficient capital to start a business. Women could also encounter discrimination in the product market.

Overall, the determinants of successful entrepreneurship are quite similar to the usual determinants of individual wages: gender, social background, education and intelligence. Risk attitude is found as an additional determinant.

In order to establish whether these structural estimates are at all robust, Table 5A.1 in the appendix gives the estimates of a reduced-form equation, namely, a standard Tobit model, where labour demand is explained by the same set of regressors without further restrictions on the coefficients. A Tobit model is estimated, rather than a standard ordinary least squares regression model (OLS), because there is a threshold value of labour demand at zero: negative values of labour demand are not feasible. On the whole, the results are quite similar. The estimates of Table 5.2 have barely been affected by the theoretical parameter restrictions of the structural model.

Summary and conclusion
This chapter explains business formation and labour demand from risk attitude and entrepreneurial ability, where the latter is modelled as a function of individual characteristics. The resulting equilibrium model is translated into an empirical structural model that explains whether one starts a business and, if so, how many people one will employ. The size of the workforce is regarded as an indicator of entrepreneurial success. The estimation results pertain to a sample of Dutch individuals for whom determinants of entrepreneurial ability as well as a measure of risk aversion have been observed. Employees working in large firms are excluded from the sample.

The results can be compared with the historical literature as discussed in Chapter 2. The findings confirm the Chapter 4 result that risk aversion is a serious impediment to entrepreneurship. This confirms the views of several authors. Cantillon ([1755] 1979) stated that a successful entrepreneur should be willing to bear risk. Say ([1803] 1971) added that a successful entrepreneur must have not only the motivation but also the ability to bear risk. And Marshall ([1890] 1930) mentioned that young risk lovers are more inclined to start up as an entrepreneur than others. The current findings do not support Schumpeter's ([1911] 1934) idea that risk bearing is not a task of the entrepreneur and that therefore risk attitude does not play any role.

The other results are consistent with Marshall's *Principles of Economics* ([1890] 1930): success in entrepreneurship requires intelligence and general ability; general ability, in turn, depends on family background, education and innate ability.

The main contribution of this chapter is that it confirms a number of determinants of successful entrepreneurship that have been obtained before by either theory or empirics, but in most cases not by both.

The major limitation is that the empirical analysis is based on several unrealistic assumptions: a single wage rate; homogeneous employee productivity; full-time employment only; and a closed economy in which all firms owe their existence to the talents of the entrepreneur. This is a serious limitation, though the same empirical results are found by means of a reduced-form empirical analysis. Second, the causality of the correlation between risk attitude and entrepreneurship is not proven, since risk attitude is measured after occupations have been chosen. I assume risk attitude to be constant over time, but I am not in a position to prove that assumption.

It is hoped that these limitations may call for further modelling and estimation so that these unrealistic assumptions may subsequently be relaxed, or a more sophisticated empirical measure of risk attitude may be made available.[16] Chapter 6 is devoted to a closer investigation of the determinants of entrepreneurship *success*.

Appendix 5A

Derivation of the threshold value of labour demand, log c_i, as in equation (5.6)
In the first period people choose an occupation by comparing the (expected) utility level associated with entrepreneurship to the utility they can derive from wage employment. This comparison leads to the choice for entrepreneurship whenever $EU_i^e \geq U_i^w$, or:

$$\log(EU_i^e) \geq \log(U_i^w). \tag{5A.1}$$

EU_i^e can be derived from (5.4), using the properties of the log-normal distribution (Mood et al., 1986, p. 117). We then take the log of the expectation and derive:

$$\log(EU_i^e) = \frac{1 - R_i}{1 - \gamma} X_i \beta + \frac{1 - R_i}{1 - \gamma} \gamma \log\left(\frac{\gamma}{w}\right)$$
$$+ (1 - R_i)\log(1 - \gamma) - \log(1 - R_i) + \frac{(1 - R_i)^2 \sigma^2}{2(1 - \gamma)^2}.$$

The right-hand side of inequality (5A.1) is given by (5.5). Solving the inequality to find a threshold value of entrepreneurial ability, that is, a minimum value of the expectation of own ability at which an individual is just willing to start up as an entrepreneur, we obtain the inequality:

$$X_i\beta \geq \log w - \gamma\log(\gamma) - (1-\gamma)\log(1-\gamma) - \frac{(1-R_i)\sigma^2}{2(1-\gamma)}, \quad (5A.2)$$

which is a necessary and sufficient condition to start up as an entrepreneur. The entrepreneurial ability required is a non-decreasing function of risk aversion and of the wage rate. This expression for the threshold value of (expected) entrepreneurial ability necessary to be willing to start up as an entrepreneur can be related to, if you will, a 'reservation labour demand' c_i. This means that individuals decide to start a business if and only if their expected labour demand exceeds c_i, owing to their specific preferences as expressed by the utility function. People choose entrepreneurship whenever $E\log \hat{L}_i \geq \log c_i$. The expected value of $\log \hat{L}_i$ follows from equation (5.3). Multiplying both sides of inequality (5A.2) by $1/(1-\gamma)$ and adding the term $[1/(1-\gamma)]\log(\gamma/w)$ results in an inequality of which the right-hand side expresses the threshold value of $E\log \hat{L}_i$, the reservation labour demand ($\log c_i$):

$$E\log \hat{L}_i \geq \frac{\sigma^2}{2(1-\gamma)^2}(R_i - 1) + \log\gamma - \log(1-\gamma) = \log c_i.$$

This is equivalent to condition (5A.1) as specified in (5A.2). The proportion of entrepreneurs in the population α equals the fraction of individuals for whom this inequality holds.

Derivation of the equilibrium wage rate, w, as in equation (5.10)
Per definition it holds that:

$$\sum_{i\in I} L_i \equiv N,$$

where I is the group of entrepreneurs, size equal to αN. This, together with equation (5.2), implies:

$$\sum_{i\in I} L_i \equiv \sum_{i\in I} \left(\frac{\gamma}{w}\right)^{1/(1-\gamma)} (\theta_i)^{1/(1-\gamma)} \equiv N.$$

And, because $E\theta_i = \exp(X_i\beta + \frac{1}{2}\sigma^2)$,

$$E\sum_{i\in I} \theta_i^{1/(1-\gamma)} = \sum_{i\in I} E\theta_i^{1/(1-\gamma)} = \sum_{i\in I} \exp\left[\frac{X_i\beta}{1-\gamma} + \frac{\sigma^2}{2(1-\gamma)^2}\right].$$

Replacing the left-hand side of equation (5.10) by its expected value gives:

$$\exp\left[\frac{\sigma^2}{2(1-\gamma)^2}\right]\sum_{i\in I}\exp\left(\frac{X_i\beta}{1-\gamma}\right) = N\left(\frac{w}{\gamma}\right)^{1/(1-\gamma)}.$$

This yields the result:

$$\log w = (1-\gamma)\log\left[\frac{\sum_{i\in I}\exp\left(\frac{X_i\beta}{1-\gamma}\right)}{N}\right] + \log\gamma + \frac{\sigma^2}{2(1-\gamma)^2}.$$

Substituting this result for log w into equation (5.7), we have:

$$\log L_i = \frac{\log\theta_i}{1-\gamma} - \log\left[\frac{\sum_{i\in I}\exp\left(\frac{X_i\beta}{1-\gamma}\right)}{N}\right] - \frac{\sigma^2}{2(1-\gamma)^2}$$

for the labour demand function.

Estimation results of the reduced-form (Tobit) model
These are included in Table 5A.1.[17]

Table 5A.1   Estimation results of a reduced-form Tobit model

Variable	Estimate	($|t$-value$|$)
Constant	−2.148	(8.64)***
Female	−1.171	(19.47)***
IQ at age 12	1.827	(7.60)***
Father self-employed	0.472	(5.57)***
Father unskilled work	−0.473	(5.19)***
Father manager	0.973	(5.90)***
Education (1–7)	0.155	(7.81)***
General, intermediate level	0.802	(9.74)***
Vocational, intermediate level	1.180	(13.93)***
Arts-oriented education	−0.688	(8.71)***
Science-oriented education	0.134	(2.03)**
Risk attitude	−0.679	(10.06)***
σ	1.71	(15.49)***
Log likelihood	−1622	

Note: Coefficients are significant at the 1% level if the corresponding absolute t-value is at least 2.58 (marked with ***), at the 5% level if the corresponding absolute t-value is at least 1.96 (marked with **).

Notes

1. There are other recent contributions to the theory of entrepreneurship which have their roots in the models discussed above. Examples are Calvo and Wellisz (1980), Jovanovic (1994) and Blanchflower and Oswald (1998).
2. The distinction of these two decisions illustrates once again how this model links Part II with Parts III and IV.
3. Returns to managerial coordination are decreasing in accordance with Kaldor (1934) and Coase (1937).
4. Necessarily, in order to represent entrepreneurship as a discrete choice, the minimum workforce of a firm is 1; we cannot allow for part-time entrepreneurship (or for part-time employment).
5. There is a technical inconsistency: L_j has earlier been defined as an integer variable while the optimal potential workforce defined here is clearly continuous. I shall return to this issue below.
6. As in Kanbur's model, the individual is motivated by expectations on the basis of the known distribution of his unknown entrepreneurial talents; but here this distribution is not the same for all individuals, but a function of their known characteristics x_i.
7. See the Appendix 5A.
8. *In the aggregate*, it is assumed that the realized value of θ (and therefore of L and π) equals its expected value. It is realized that the resulting labour demand slightly underestimates the true labour demand, since we do not correct for the cases where the true labour demand is below 1. The underestimate is quantified below.
9. The data do not permit an analysis in which individual employee wages are included: occupational choices pertain to various years. Wage data are available for 1983 and 1993 only.
10. The non-integer outcomes of $L_j > 1$, which are assumed to be integer, are supposed to cause no serious problem estimation errors: over- and underestimates most probably cancel each other out.
11. The same data set was employed in Chapter 4. A more extensive description of the origins of the data can be found in that chapter.
12. For entrepreneurs who are still in business in 1993, the recorded number is of course the minimum of the maximum size they will ever attain.
13. Obviously, the fact that risk attitude is assessed in an interview, in most cases many years after the entrepreneurship decision has been taken, is a disadvantage. While we use the reported variable in retrospect to explain the entrepreneurship decision, the true causality between the two is unclear; see also Chapter 4.
14. As I is endogenous, a manual iteration procedure was used to substitute μ in the likelihood function. Starting from an arbitrary value, iterations proceeded until the calculated μ was equal to the input value.
15. Variables that were found insignificant are: parental education level, family status and parental household composition; skills, as measured by knowledge and comprehension tests while in school.
16. The latter, that is, finding a better empirical measure of risk attitude, has already been developed by Ekelund et al. (2000).
17. The point of truncation is 0. R_i, risk attitude, is included as a simple regressor; since I here establish its effect on labour demand, not on reservation labour demand, this should be reversed in sign. Otherwise the results are directly comparable with those of Table 5.2. The log likelihood of the Tobit model is higher than that of the structural model. But since the two models are not nested, the likelihood ratio test does not apply.

6   Survival and success of entrepreneurs*

> The requisite capacity and talent limit the number of competitors for the business of entrepreneurs. Nor is this all: there is always a degree of risk attending such undertakings; however well they may be conducted, there is a chance of failure; the entrepreneur may, without any fault of his own, sink his fortune, and in some measure his character. (Say [1803] 1971, p. 331)

Introduction

An effective government policy to decrease unemployment is to stimulate the number of new businesses. A well-known problem with new businesses is their high dissolution rate. Of every 100 start-ups, only 50 firms survive the first three years. Hence, authorities should not only stimulate business start-ups, but also strive to minimize the number of business dissolutions. It is therefore highly relevant to investigate and understand the individual determinants of business survival.

Business survival determinants are not only interesting to authorities. Commercially oriented institutions involved in new businesses, for example banks, might benefit from understanding these determinants as well when the determinants are used for the decision as to which starting enterprises should be supported with a loan.

The objective of this chapter is to quantify the *person*-specific determinants of survival duration and of success in business. I focus on the person- rather than on the business-specific determinants because I presume that it is the man who makes the difference: he sets the conditions, the boundaries, the characteristics and, ultimately the value-creating ability of the newly founded firm. Chandler and Hanks (1994), Peteraf and Shanley (1997) and Reuber and Fischer (1999) explicitly mention that for new ventures, the firm can be considered to be an extension of the founder. Nicholas Kaldor (1934, pp. 69–70), had already put this as follows:

> On this definition, firms whose coordinating ability changes, while preserving their legal identity, would not remain the same firms; but then all the theoretically relevant characteristics of a firm change with changes in coordinating ability. It might as well be treated, therefore, as a different firm.

This focus on the individual as the level of analysis also enables us to cope with the growing recognition that entrepreneurship may be a 'habitus' rather than a single-event action (Wright and Westhead, 1998). The unit of analysis in a person-oriented *duration* analysis is the duration in business of the individual, not of the venture. Exits are associated with moving out of self-employment to (un)employment. I use the terms 'entrepreneur' and 'self-employed' as synonyms.

Quantification of the person-specific determinants of survival duration and of success in business is achieved by estimating a duration model on a sample consisting of young males who became entrepreneurs between 1985 and 1989. Actually, I consider these individuals from the sample of Chapter 3 who have ever shown that they had sufficient opportunity and willingness to become an entrepreneur in the period studied.

The performance measure (of success) I look at in this study is unique and is mostly related to business duration. I argue that the mere measurement of business duration could have little relationship with success in business, since a large part of business dissolutions is voluntary (see the data section for its frequency). The present study uses an alternative, and in my opinion more appropriate, definition of success in business. This definition is enabled by the estimation of a model that distinguishes among compulsory exits from the entrepreneurs' community, failures and voluntary exits. Estimating such a competing risks model is possible since the data are informative about exit routes. Only compulsory exits are associated with lack of success. In this manner, person-oriented determinants of successful entrepreneurship can be estimated. The exact definition of business success is given below, along with a few others.

A *compulsory exit*, after, say, a period of length T in business, is due to a lack of sufficient (financial) opportunity to continue in business. This exit route is associated with *business failure*. A *voluntary exit* after a period of length T in business, on the other hand, is due to a lack of willingness or motivation to continue in business. A better outside option is encountered in the labour market, evidently before the business owner is forced to exit. *Business dissolution* can be either a voluntary or a compulsory exit out of entrepreneurship. The *business survival duration* is defined as the (at $t = 0$) expected period of length T in business, which will eventually end in either of the exit routes out of self-employment. The indicator for *business success* is the (at $t = 0$) expected period of length T' in business after eliminating the voluntary exit route (thereby treating voluntary exits as right censored observations). Hence, only compulsory exits are considered in measuring business success; the longer T', the more successful is the entrepreneur.

In line with these definitions, estimating the single-risk model renders the determinants of business survival. Estimating the competing risks model leads to measuring individual success determinants together with the determinants of 'motivation' to continue in business.

The chapter is organized as follows. The next section deals with the choice of explanatory variables. The following section describes the sample. Subsequently, the model, the estimation results and conclusions are discussed.

Determinants of survival and success in business
The objective of this section is to derive from either theory or empirical research hypotheses about the determinants of survival and success in business. The potential regressor variables of the aggregate model explaining business survival are derived in the subsection below.

In the subsection that follows, the success determinants to be used in the competing risks model are assembled. As quantitative empirical evidence on the direct determinants of success in business is relatively scarce and since a rich historical knowledge base about successful entrepreneurship exists (see Chapter 2), I derived these success determinants by reviewing these important historical contributions to the theory of entrepreneurship. I translated the relevant ideas of Jean-Baptiste Say, Alfred Marshall, Joseph Schumpeter and Frank Knight into empirically useful success determinants (see Tables 2.1 and 2.2).

Determinants of survival in business
There is relatively little theoretical or empirical literature about the person-specific determinants of the duration of a business venture. Among the exceptions are Brüderl et al. (1992), Cooper et al. (1994) and Pennings et al. (1998) as well as the application in Chapter 8. However, there is ample empirical evidence that points to the effect of person-specific regressor variables on the probabilities of:

- becoming self-employed in a certain period, Pr(Inflow): $\Pr(IF)$;
- exiting self-employment in a certain period, Pr(Outflow): $\Pr(OF)$; and
- being part of the stock of self-employed at a certain moment: $\Pr(SE)$.

Combining the empirical evidence pertaining to these probabilities by means of a simple statistical relationship developed for this purpose (see subsection below), results in hypotheses about the qualitative effect of regressor variables on self-employment duration, the dependent variable in the aggregate model.

Statistical relationship: inflow, stock and duration   Suppose that the total inflow into the stock of entrepreneurs is equal to the total outflow and that the economy is in a steady state, such that:

$$\log[\mathrm{E}(T)] = \log[\Pr(SE)] - \log[\Pr(IF)], \qquad (6.1)$$

where E(*T*) is the mean (completed) self-employment duration (in months).[1] I wish to derive the relationships between the effects of particular regressor variables on these quantities. Whereas it is possible to observe for each entrepreneur within a sample the (in)complete duration of his (individual) venture, it is not possible to observe the *probabilities* Pr(*SE*) and Pr(*IF*) of equation (6.1) for each individual. I observe only the dichotomous outcome of the individual to be self-employed (*SE*) or to become self-employed (*IF*). The dichotomies are explained by sets of regressor variables. The predicted values of Pr(*SE*) and Pr(*IF*) can be calculated for each individual by means of the regression equation.

For the moment it is assumed that Pr(*SE*) and Pr(*IF*) are explained by the same set of regressor variables. Denote the *j*th element of the set of regressor variables **x** by x_j. Taking partial derivatives with respect to x_j in equation (6.1) renders:

$$\gamma_j = \frac{\partial}{\partial x_j}\log[E(T)] = \frac{1}{\Pr(SE)} * [\phi(\mathbf{x}'\beta_{SE})\beta_{SE}^j - \phi(\mathbf{x}'\beta_{IF})\beta_{IF}^j E(T)], \quad (6.2)$$

where β_{SE} and β_{IF} denote vectors of parameters and where Pr(*SE*) and Pr(*IF*) are a function of $\mathbf{x}'\beta_{SE}$ and $\mathbf{x}'\beta_{IF}$, respectively. β_{SE}^j and β_{IF}^j denote the *j*th elements of the parameter vectors and correspond to the effect of x_j on the respective probabilities. Finally, ϕ depends on the specification applied and is non-negative.

Equation (6.2) reduces to a numerical expression for the predicted effect of each particular regressor on log[E(*T*)], the expected length of business survival, if (average) sample characteristics are known along with the parameter estimates. Consequently, imputing the already existing empirical evidence about the coefficients β_{SE}^j and β_{IF}^j into this relationship renders the hypotheses that we are seeking, the expected effect of x_j on business survival.

I shall cautiously restrict the predictions to the *qualitative* effect of a regressor on E(*T*). This caution is appropriate not only because of the strict assumptions underlying equation (6.1), but also because I establish the predicted effects on the basis of estimated βs from different samples, derived in various models with different sets of regressor variables. Table 6.1 results from inserting all possible combinations of positive, negative and zero β_{SE}s and β_{IF}s into equation (6.2). It serves as a theoretical a priori table. Applying the relation of equation (6.2) to already existing empirical evidence about Pr(*SE*) and Pr(*IF*) leads to a framework which can be used as a tool for the selection of regressor variables.

The interpretation of Table 6.1 can be intuitively clarified. Suppose that we are looking for a hypothesis about the effect of former entrepreneurship experience on the hazard of self-employment. Moreover, suppose that we

Table 6.1   Predicted sign of γ, the hazard rate, given the signs of β_{SE} and β_{IF}

Sign of	$\rightarrow$ $+$	β_{SE} 0	$\rightarrow$ $-$
$\downarrow$ $\quad$ $+$	?	–	–
β_{IF} $\quad$ 0	+	0	–
$\downarrow$ $\quad$ $-$	+	+	?

Note: The interpretation of the table is given in the text.

have some empirical evidence about the effect of this variable on the probability that someone *is* self-employed, β_{SE}, as well as on the probability that someone has switched to self-employment, β_{IF}. The probability that one is found to be self-employed is a combination of the probability that one has become self-employed ($\mathrm{Pr}(IF)$) and that one has remained so (duration). So if, for instance, former self-employment experience affects $\mathrm{Pr}(SE)$ positively, then it should affect positively the probability of starting or the probability of remaining self-employed or both. If former experience is simultaneously known to affect the probability of becoming self-employed, $\mathrm{Pr}(IF)$, insignificantly or even negatively, then we can conjecture by means of the logic developed above that entrepreneurship experience increases duration (and decreases the hazard of entrepreneurship).

Outflow and duration   Binary outflow studies explain a (time-independent) hazard of exit from self-employment during a certain time interval. Thus, it may simply be stated that the estimated effect of regressors on exit, β_{OF} and on duration have reverse signs, apart from the effect of time-varying covariates.

The empirical relationships   The relevant empirical evidence pertaining to $\mathrm{Pr}(IF)$, $\mathrm{Pr}(SE)$, $\mathrm{Pr}(OF)$ and $E(T)$ has been classified in Table 6.2.[2] It contains variables that will be included in the model that explains individual self-employment durations.

Determinants of success in business
Since the relevant parts of entrepreneurship theories by Schumpeter, Marshall, Say and Knight have seldom been put to an empirical test, it is an interesting exercise to do so using the current data. I shall basically use the classic theoretical knowledge base to obtain hypotheses on the determinants of successful entrepreneurship. These have been provided in Table 2.2 in Chapter 2.

Table 6.2   *Summary of existing evidence on* β_{IF}, β_{SE}, β_{OF} *and* γ

Variable	Pr(Inflow)		Pr(Stock)		Pr(Outflow)		E(T)
	US	other	US	Other	US	other	Europe
Age	0	+	+	+	−	0	n/a
Age squared	0	−	−	−	+	n/a	n/a
Education	0	−	+/0	+/0	?	+	+
Handicap (dummy)	0	n/a	?	−	n/a	n/a	n/a
Veteran (dummy)	−	n/a	+	n/a	n/a	n/a	n/a
(Wage) experience	0	n/a	+	0	?	?	+
Industry experience	n/a	n/a	n/a	n/a	n/a	n/a	+
Self-employment expr.	+	n/a	n/a	n/a	n/a	n/a	0
Unemployment (expr.)	+/0	+	+	n/a	n/a	n/a	n/a
Job changes	0/+	0	+	n/a	n/a	n/a	n/a
Children	−	n/a	+	0	0	n/a	n/a
Married (dummy)	?	0	0	0	0	0	n/a
Urban (dummy)	0	n/a	−	n/a	n/a	n/a	n/a
Rotter score (dummy)	0	n/a	+	n/a	n/a	n/a	n/a
Assets	+	n/a	n/a	+	−	n/a	n/a
Assets squared	0	n/a	n/a	n/a	+	n/a	n/a
Home owner (dummy)	0/+	n/a	n/a	n/a	+	n/a	n/a
Income	0/−	n/a	n/a	n/a	0	n/a	n/a
Industry dummies							
Agriculture	+	+	n/a	+	0	0	n/a
Trade	+	n/a	n/a	n/a	0	n/a	−
Business/repair	0	n/a	n/a	+	0	n/a	n/a
Personal services	+	n/a	n/a	n/a	0	n/a	n/a
Transport/communic.	0	−	n/a	n/a	0	0	−
Occupation dummies							
Professional	n/a	0	+	n/a	n/a	0	n/a
Manager	0	0	+	n/a	+	n/a	n/a
Sales	n/a	−	+	n/a	n/a	n/a	n/a
Craft	n/a	n/a	+	n/a	n/a	n/a	n/a
Farmer	0	0	+	n/a	0	n/a	n/a
No. of co-founders							+

Notes:
The entries in the table should be interpreted as follows:
+ (−)   A positive (negative) effect was found in all the empirical studies available.
0   An insignificant effect was found in all the empirical studies available.
+ (−)/0   Some studies report a positive (negative), some a zero effect.
?   Some studies report a positive, some a negative effect.
n/a   Not included in any study.
The studies reported in Chapters 7 and 8 have not been included in this table.

A comparison of these classical views on the capability, conduct, attitude and asset ownership required for the successful business founder leads to some observations on how they complement and partly contradict one another. Say and Marshall both give much weight to certain abilities related to the managing function of the business founder. They also stress capabilities related to leadership and industry-specific abilities. Schumpeter, who stresses the leadership function of the business founder (but considers the managerial function as irrelevant), emphasizes a certain attitude, a willingness to show deviating behaviour. Psychological factors are much more important than human capital factors, according to Schumpeter. His view thereby almost completely contradicts the (neo)classical views of Say and Marshall. Knight integrates (Schumpeter's) psychological requirements into the (neo)classical ability requirements. On the other hand, Say and Schumpeter agree that capital ownership is not a requirement for successful business ownership, thereby contradicting Marshall's and Knight's view that capital ownership *is* a factor affecting performance.

These determinants of business failure and success will be tested empirically along with the determinants of voluntary business dissolutions due to a lack of motivation to continue in business. The latter is assumed to depend on variables that determine both the accessibility and the desirability of outside options such as general experience, age and education.

Data

The sample is drawn from the National Longitudinal Survey of Youth (NLSY79) and is very similar to the subsample of entrepreneurs in the study of Chapter 3: the first interview among the approximately 12 000 respondents was held in 1979 when they were between 14 and 22 years old. Since then, these extensive interviews have been repeated annually. The last available year for this study is 1989. I use a subsample of white males for homogeneity reasons. All observed switches to self-employment are sampled and for these the duration of the self-employment spell is recorded. This results in a sample of 271 observed durations in self-employment where the self-employed are white males aged 20 to 32 who have become self-employed in their own (un)incorporated businesses between 1985 and 1989. Some 145 observations were right censored; these young men were still self-employed at their last interview. Note that inflow into the class of self-employed took place continuously during the time interval under analysis. As a consequence, the observed duration of right-censored observations may be anything between one month and five years.

Although interviews took place at intervals of approximately a year, the duration variable used is measured in months and treated as continuous. This smaller unit of measurement has been obtained by utilization of employer supplements for every observation each survey year. This search also provided the opportunity to ascertain whether exits were voluntary or compulsory. The survey includes a question to people who terminated a particular occupation (either employed or self-employed) about the reason for termination. I consider the categories 'bankruptcy of the firm' and 'fired' as compulsory. Although phrasing of reasons for terminating a job is not particularly suitable for self-employed persons in the NLSY, the question applies to them too. 'Quits' and the like are considered as voluntary exits. There is perhaps a natural tendency to report an exit as voluntary versus compulsory. I therefore treat 'voluntary' exits as compulsory whenever they are succeeded by a period of compulsory unemployment of at least two months, where two months is an arbitrary choice.

The 126 observed exits are divided into 55 (44 per cent) compulsory and 71 (56 per cent) voluntary exits. Of course, the choice and interpretation of this variable is open to criticism. Fortunately, I shall have an opportunity to verify whether the usage of this variable to discriminate among two different exit routes makes sense: I shall check empirically whether the two alternatives differ significantly from each other. If they do, it would be quite improbable that the source of the information on exit routes, the answers to a particular (and quite unclear) question from the questionnaire, is completely unreliable.

A wide variety of potential exogenous variables are included in the NLSY79. However, an adequate indicator of business conditions is not included. An indicator of macroeconomic business conditions is a potentially important regressor variable in a business hazard equation. The 1992 Statistical Abstract of the United States Databook is used to remedy this omission. One macroeconomic indicator is the business failure rate that measures the number of business failures per 10 000 concerns by industry for each calendar year. This variable has been included as a macroeconomic time-varying covariate together with the unemployment rate. They both capture variations in general business conditions.

All other exogenous variables are treated as time independent and are included in the NLSY79. These variables take on the values that are reported during the last interview prior to the switch to entrepreneurship. This decision rule aims at preventing problems with endogeneity. Industry and occupation dummies are, however, recorded after the switch to self-employment.

Model

The appropriate method to study durations of any kind is estimating a survival model. As in an ordinary least squares (OLS) regression model, a dependent variable is explained by means of a set of independent regressor variables. Survival models deviate a little from OLS models due to some unique features of the problem for which they are employed. Durations are explained and it might be possible and it is actually the case in the current application that the values of some independent variables vary over that time period. Survival or hazard models can cope with that variation. Furthermore, one should also be able to deal with the possibility that the hazard itself (the dependent variable of the model) varies over time. Survival models as employed here are able to deal with that aspect too.

In the survival model, T is defined as a continuous random variable denoting the number of months a small business owner remains in business.[3] Time as it passes is denoted by t in the model, irrespective of calendar time. Hence, all entrepreneurs start their businesses at $t=0$. The probability density function of T is $f(t)$, its distribution function $F(t)$. The survivor function is defined as $S(t)=1-F(t)=\Pr(T\geq t)$. The hazard $\theta(t)$ specifies the (conditional) probability that someone, who has remained in business for a period from 0 to t, exits in the short interval $(t, t+dt)$, and is defined as (see Lancaster 1992, p. 8).

$$\theta(t) = \frac{f(t)}{S(t)}. \tag{6.3}$$

The hazard function is modelled as a function of a set of exogenous person-specific regressors, the vector $\mathbf{x}$, and of time t to permit duration dependence. Assuming the absence of regressors, the hazard is a non-monotonic function of t. The assumption was shown to hold by a first inspection of the duration data. A simple hazard specification that permits non-monotonic behaviour is the log logistic (see ibid., p. 44),

$$\theta(t,\mathbf{x}) = \frac{k(\mathbf{x})\alpha t^{\alpha-1}}{1 + k(\mathbf{x})t^{\alpha}}. \tag{6.4}$$

I specify $k(\mathbf{x}) = \exp(\mathbf{x}'\beta)$. Given this, taking the partial derivative of equation (6.4) with respect to a regressor x_j, and rearranging, I obtain:

$$\beta_j = [S(t,\mathbf{x})]^{-1}\frac{\partial\log\theta(t,\mathbf{x})}{\partial x_j}, \tag{6.5}$$

where:

$$S(t,\mathbf{x}) = \exp[-\int_0^t \theta(s,\mathbf{x})ds] = [1 + k(\mathbf{x})t^{\alpha}]^{-1},$$

and:

$$\log\theta(t,\mathbf{x}) = \mathbf{x}'\beta + \log\alpha + (\alpha - 1)\log t - \log[1 + \exp(\mathbf{x}'\beta)t^{\alpha}],$$

thus giving the proportional effect of each explanatory variable on the conditional probability of leaving self-employment.

Consequently,

$$\gamma_j = \frac{\partial \log(T)}{\partial x_j} = -\frac{\beta_j}{\alpha}. \tag{6.6}$$

This equation specifies the relationship between the β_j's found when estimating the hazard function $\theta(t,\mathbf{x})$ and the γ_j's resulting from estimation of $\log(T)$ and which are referred to in Tables 6.1 and 6.2.

I modify $\mathbf{x}$ to $\mathbf{x}(t_c)$ to permit the inclusion of (calendar!) time-varying regressors; the macroeconomic indicators of business conditions. These conditions vary over both calendar time and observations.[4] The danger of unacknowledged endogeneity pertaining to time-varying covariates is obviously absent in this particular application. The sample is taken from the flow of entrants to the state 'self-employment'. Since this sampling scheme is uninformative about t, the log likelihood to be maximized is as follows:

$$L_i = d_i \log \theta_i(t_i) - \int_0^{t_i} \theta_i(u)\,du, \tag{6.7}$$

where $d_i = 1$ if individual i's exit is observed at t_i and $d_i = 0$ if i's length of time in business is right censored. The parameter estimates resulting from maximizing this likelihood are denoted as the results of *Model I*, the single-destination or single-risk model.

In the second model, *Model II*, I utilize the available information on destinations after business dissolution. I allow for different hazards: θ_w, the hazard for a transition due to a lack of willingness to continue in self-employment; and θ_o, the hazard for exiting the self-employment state due to a lack of opportunity to continue. This approach to modelling multiple destinations is referred to as a *competing-risks model*. I adopt it as Model II where $\theta(t) = \theta_w(t) + \theta_o(t)$.

Define M^* as the number of destinations that is parametrically specified and d_{im} as a dummy variable equal to one if individual i is observed to make a transition to state m and zero otherwise. Lancaster (ibid.,p. 162) derives the log likelihood as:

$$L = \sum_{m \in M^*} L_m, \tag{6.8}$$

where:

$$L_m = \sum_{i=1}^{N} [d_{im} \log \theta_{im}(t_i) - \int_0^{t_{im}} \theta_{im}(u)\,du]. \tag{6.9}$$

This representation of the problem is a great simplification as the problem may be decomposed into a set of M* different subproblems with a single destination, and right censoring for all observations that did not reach this destination. The estimators of all subproblems are distributed independently.

I shall test whether the two specified hazards are statistically distinct or whether the competing-risks model reduces to the single-risk model. I do so by means of a likelihood ratio test as in Lindeboom and Theeuwes (1991). As noted before, this test also gives insight into the validity and discriminating power of the empirical measure for exit routes.

Finally, I shall not formally test for the presence of unobserved heterogeneity. The reason is that many complications arise due to the inclusion of time-varying regressors. I excluded these regressors in order to test for the presence of unobserved heterogeneity by means of introducing a Gamma mixing distribution. However, I did not find evidence of unobserved heterogeneity.

Estimation results

Table 6.3 shows the estimation results. The first column pertains to the single-risk model, the others to the competing-risks model. The hazard for a transition to any state out of the self-employment state is denoted by θ, where θ depends on individual-specific covariates and time. The hazard for a transition to 'compulsory exit' is denoted by θ_o, while θ_w denotes the hazard for voluntary exits. To obtain estimated effects of regressors on log duration, reverse the sign of the given parameter estimate and divide by $\hat{\alpha}$.

Age

Table 6.3 shows that age affects all hazards (significantly) negatively: the older one is at the time one first starts up as an entrepreneur, the longer one survives (the lower the hazard). The lower hazard in the single-risk model is shown to be a combined effect: both voluntary and forced exits are more probable for business owners who started at a younger age. The variable 'age squared' is an additional significant factor for explaining the hazard of compulsory exit. The total effect is as follows: age affects the hazard negatively below a starting age of 32. Above that age, the effect is positive. The optimal starting age would therefore be 32. However, the current finding pertains only to an age group between 20 and 32. Therefore, the only observed part is the negative effect. This result was obtained while controlling for experience.

The effect of the variable 'age' on the hazards of the competing-risks model, θ_o and θ_w, might shed some light on the source of the relative

Table 6.3   Estimation results of the hazard model of self-employment

	Single risk		Competing risks			
	θ	(|t − value|)	θ_o	(|t − value|)	θ_w	(|t − value|)
$\hat{\alpha}$	2.37	(10.67)	1.91	(5.96)	2.35	(8.11)
Human capital variables						
Age	−0.41	(2.78)***	−0.57	(2.71)***	−0.39	(2.20)**
(Age squared)/10	0.05	(1.43)	0.09	(1.73)*	0.05	(1.06)
Labour experience	0.11	(1.45)	−0.04	(0.37)	0.25	(2.45)**
Within-industry experience	−0.30	(3.14)***	−0.25	(1.96)**	−0.29	(2.33)**
Within-occupation experience	−0.64	(1.92)*	−0.37	(0.80)	−0.61	(1.59)
Experience in self-employment	−0.13	(0.99)	−0.07	(0.39)	−0.16	(0.84)
Financial variables						
Assets ($1000) prior to start	−0.00	(0.17)	−0.00	(0.23)	−0.00	(0.15)
Home owner (dummy)	−0.62	(1.58)	−0.44	(0.86)	−0.58	(1.19)
Motivations at the start						
Started while unemployed	0.85	(2.35)**	1.15	(2.42)**	0.11	(0.25)
Started during employment	−0.55	(1.86)*	−0.01	(0.02)	−0.86	(1.81)*

Industry dummies						
Agriculture	−2.88	(5.47)***	−2.52	(3.35)***	−2.55	(3.92)***
Business and repair services	−1.09	(3.17)***	−0.51	(1.20)	−1.69	(3.44)***
Macroeconomic variables						
Unemployment rate^t	−0.35	(1.23)	−0.27	(0.74)	−0.32	(0.90)
Business failure rate^t	0.03	(6.07)***	0.03	(5.25)***	0.02	(3.41)***
Minus log likelihood	532		602			
Estimated median (months)	23.8		46.5		33.5	
Sample median (months)	24.3		57.0		42.5	

Note: Coefficients are significant at the 1% level if the corresponding absolute *t*-value is at least 2.58 (marked with ***), at the 5% level if the corresponding absolute *t*-value is at least 1.96 (marked with **). They are marginally significant (at the 10% level) if the corresponding *t*-value is at least 1.65 (marked with *). ^{t} denotes a variable to be time-varying.

disadvantage of very young entrepreneurs. As is deduced from the negative coefficient of age in the θ_w equation, the very young starters from this sample are more likely than the more mature ones to find (better) outside opportunities and thereby exit voluntarily. The also negative coefficient of age in the θ_o equation shows that these youngsters are also more likely to fail due to a lack of leadership or 'knowledge of the world' as Schumpeter, Say and Marshall put it (see Table 2.2).

These results are also largely consistent with expectations based on Table 6.2. The empirical evidence for the United States shows that age does not affect the probability of *becoming* self-employed, while older people face a significant higher probability of belonging to the pool of self-employed, and a lower probability of exiting the self-employment status. Combining this with Table 6.1 leads to the hypothesis that age affects θ negatively and duration positively. The result in the first column of Table 6.3 confirms the hypothesis based on empirical evidence: younger starters have lower survival probabilities than older ones. The fact that this is mainly a consequence of an increased hazard of compulsory exit is in accordance with the classical economists.

Experience

Experience in the same industry as the business venture gives better chances, and so does experience within the same occupation. Experience in the industry affects all hazards significantly negatively. Experience in the occupation becomes significant only as a combined effect of compulsory and voluntary exits. These findings are consistent with the collected evidence (see Tables 6.2 and 2.2) that relevant experience helps one to become a successful business owner (and to survive). They also support (especially Say's) classical theory.

Another estimate in line with the collected evidence, but contradicting common belief, is the effect of former self-employment experience on business survival.[5] Experience in self-employment does not significantly influence the length of a business venture, nor does it alter the hazard rate of compulsory exit. The latter effect, though, was expected, based on empirical findings.

The zero effect of the regressor 'general labour experience' (in years) contradicts the empirical evidence (Table 6.2 suggests a negative effect of experience in wage employment on θ). The most interesting part of the findings with respect to general labour experience is its positive effect on the hazard for voluntary exits. General labour market experience increases the hazard for voluntary exits significantly. The more labour experience, the more outside options one has, and the higher will be the probability that these options compare favourably with self-employment. General labour market experience does not influence success or failure in business. The experience is apparently not to be classified as 'relevant', unlike experience in the same industry as the new venture.

Financial variables

Parameter estimates for financial variables are insignificant in all three equations. People starting with their own capital are as successful as those who start with debt capital. Although banks take great care in selecting entrepreneurs to whom they grant a loan, they have not succeeded in making this group any more successful than the group of entrepreneurs starting with their own business capital. This result is consistent with Table 6.2 (as long as one does not consider coefficients in the exit equation that are estimated from a sample of inheritance receivers, Holtz-Eakin et al., 1994a). It does, however, contradict the more recent evidence on success determinants (see Chapter 8). The classical theories of Marshall and Knight are also rejected by this application. Say and Schumpeter have already argued that own capital should not be an issue (in a perfect and complete capital market).

Motivation to start a business

The type of incentive that people experience to start a business has a strong influence on θ. Young men who start a business while or perhaps because they are unemployed have a higher propensity to leave this state at any moment.[6] And well-prepared young Americans, who had already started their business (on a part-time basis) while they were employees, have a better chance of persevering. The pull factors generate far higher survival probabilities than the push factors. We shall come across the same type of evidence in Chapters 8 and 9.

The competing-risks model obviously sheds light on this result. Men who have started while unemployed are significantly less successful in their business ventures. They fail before they find another opportunity in the labour market as shown by the far higher coefficient in the compulsory than in the voluntary exit equation. Males who started their business while they were still employed have a significantly lower (than average) hazard of exit. This lower hazard of exit is caused by a lower probability of voluntary exit. Hence, this latter distinction selects the entrepreneurs most motivated to continue rather than those who are the most successful.

Industry dummies and macroeconomic variables

All industry dummies turned out to be insignificant, except for the industries listed in Table 6.3. Starting a business in the agricultural or business and repair services industries affects the survival probability of the entrepreneur. These industries have a negative effect on the hazard. Note that the time-varying covariate 'business failure rate' (not yet discussed) varies over industries, is highly significant, and was not part of any previous study.[7]

It is notable that the industry 'business and repair services' decreases θ through its positive effect on 'willingness to continue'. While failure perspectives are average within this industry (the coefficient in the θ_o equation is not significantly different from zero), the motivation to continue in business is significantly higher. Outside options appear to be significantly less attractive or accessible in this industry compared with one's current position.

The (calendar) time-varying unemployment rate does not affect duration in self-employment. The business failure rate measures the number of business failures per 10 000 existing concerns for each industry and every year. A very significant relationship exists between the business failure rate and hazard rates; the higher the business failure rate, the higher the individual hazard of self-employment. Surprisingly, macroeconomic variables are scarcely used in this type of study; and this highly significant indicator of business conditions has not been used before. Controlling for such a significant macroeconomic source of variance markedly increases the quality of results pertaining to individual effects.

The business failure rate affects not only θ_o, but also θ_w, though to a lesser extent. Poor business conditions apparently decrease the relative attractiveness of remaining self-employed, compared with outside options.

Insignificant results
The absence of several variables from Table 6.3 in the analysis should be noted. Due to the relatively small number of observations, I was not in a position to insert all regressor variables simultaneously. I opted for including all variables mentioned in Tables 2.2 and 6.2 gradually, and excluding them if their results were insignificant. Some insignificant results, which I consider of interest to report explicitly in Table 6.3, are the exception.

Excluded variables (mentioned in Table 6.2 but not in Table 6.3) are those measuring parental background, such as the educational and job levels of father and mother, as well as information concerning the composition and home language of the entrepreneur's family. Moreover, the business founder's own family situation was recorded, his education level as well as the state of his health. In addition, some other characteristics of labour market history (such as military experience, number of job changes and experience in the public sector) all had an insignificant impact on the hazard of entrepreneurship. The potential effect of three psychological measures was measured. Social psychologists believe strongly that a measure of internality of an individual's locus-of-control beliefs is a determinant of successful entrepreneurship. The Rotter scale (Rotter, 1966) is such a measure. The lower an individual's score on the Rotter scale, the less internal are his locus-of-control beliefs and the more he perceives the outcome of an event as beyond his personal control (see also Chapter 3). The dichotomous Rotter-scale measure derived from the current data set is equal to 1 for more internal individuals. It turned out to be insignificant. Because I interpreted the Rotter score as a proxy for Knight's variable 'disposition to act', this insignificant effect also contradicts Knight's theory relevant to this item. The same insignificant outcome was obtained for a related dummy that differentiates men who were extremely extroverted children from the more reserved ones. Knight's conjecture concerning the effect of 'self-confidence' was tested by means of the available information on 'self-esteem'. This turned out to have an insignificant effect on entrepreneurial success.

Moreover, location variables (Urban or SMSA dummies), and business characteristics such as number of co-starters, industry and occupational category of the business also appeared to be insignificant for the explanation of business survival and success, defined in this way.

Comparison of the (historical) success indicators to the results for θ_0
The current US situation fits the ideas of Say, Marshall, Schumpeter and Knight remarkably well.[8] On the whole, Marshall's ideas deviate the most. Education, capital and family background are all insignificant in the analysis. The insignificant results for the Rotter score (a measure for internal-locus-of-control beliefs) and for self-esteem contradict the views of Schumpeter and Knight. The industries 'agriculture' and 'business and repair' are Knight's 'easy industries' in so far as they satisfy the more basic human needs.

Duration dependence
Figure 6.1 shows how the estimated (aggregate) hazard function varies with time in business. θ increases from zero at the origin to a maximum at 27 months and then approaches zero as $t \to \infty$. The probability of surviving is high in the first period; new business owners do not give up that easily. From there, with less than 27 months in business, the probability to exit entrepreneurship increases. When people are settled in business (after more than two years) the probability to stay a business owner increases. This declining part of the hazard curve is qualitatively consistent with Jovanovic's (1982) Bayesian learning theory, which implies that a business owner learns 'on the job' how to become a better one and thereby how to increase his chances of survival.

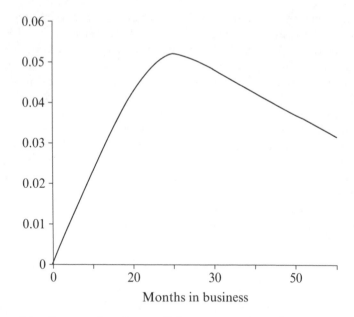

Figure 6.1 Parametric estimate of the aggregate hazard rate

Figures 6.2 and 6.3 show how the competing-risks model behaves over time. The estimated median duration if voluntary exits do not exist is 46.5 months (with a standard error of 7.1). On the other hand, when looking only at voluntary exits, assuming that business failures do not occur, the estimated median duration in business is 33.5 months (with a standard error of 3.0). It is logical that the estimated median duration increases whenever one of the two exit routes is assumed away. For instance, if voluntary exits did not occur, then every entrepreneur continues with this activity up until failure. This is due to the fact that the realized voluntary exits that are assumed away would always have occurred before the expected date of compulsory exit. Because all αs are significantly larger than 1, all θs have an inverse U-shaped relation with time; the three peaks are at 27, 44 and 38 months, respectively.

Goodness of fit
The estimated median duration of self-employment ventures is 23.8 months (standard error = 1.5). The sample median of 24.3 clearly lies within the confidence interval of the estimate. The robustness of the parameter estimates is striking. Whatever functional form is assumed or whichever set of regressors I include, the parameter estimates show little variation. Moreover, the hazards for compulsory and voluntary transitions

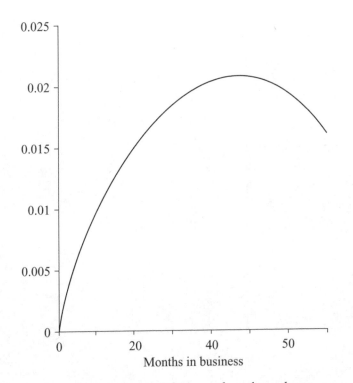

Figure 6.2   Parametric estimate of the compulsory hazard rate

can be proven to be statistically distinct.[9] The competing-risks model adds value.

Predicted durations and sensitivity analysis
Table 6.4 shows the variation in mean predicted durations upon changes in the values of several significant regressors. It shows predicted durations rather than predicted hazard rates because the latter depend also on time.[10] The predicted durations for the reference individual of Table 6.4 are shown in the second row.

These values pertain to a male individual with an average amount of assets, average education, average age and experiences (in self-employment, the industry, the occupation and in general) and who works in a region within a sector and year with average unemployment and business failure rates. He was employed prior to his start in business but did not hold a job during the start. He had no real estate and his business is in neither the agricultural sector nor the business and repair sector. The predicted duration of self-employment is 18 months.

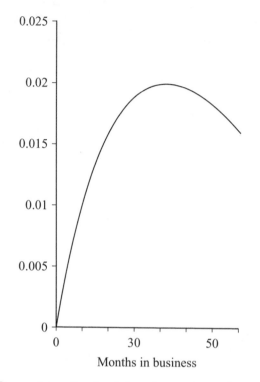

Figure 6.3   Parametric estimate of the voluntary hazard rate

If, however, voluntary exits are excluded (treated as censored) and the only remaining risk is 'compulsory exit', then the expected lifetime of his venture is much longer: 41 months. On the other hand, if compulsory exits are left out, the predicted duration of self-employment is nearly two years.

The other rows in Table 6.4 indicate the sensitivity of duration to changes in the various exogenous variables. Note that industry experience has a clear positive influence on the predicted duration, especially because experience in the industry decreases the probability of business failure. Furthermore, a low business failure rate is a very important external circumstance for low individual failure probabilities. Young men working in the agricultural sector face a(n almost implausible) longer predicted duration in business, due to the fact that both of the competing risks are lower. An unemployed young man faces a lower predicted duration in self-employment than his working counterpart mainly because unemployment prior to the start increases the likelihood of failure. General experience changes the predicted duration in the second column favourably. However, it has the opposite effect

Table 6.4   Predicted business durations (in months)

Values of exogenous variables	Both exit risks present	Compulsory exits	Voluntary exits
1. Sample means	23.8	46.5	33.5
2. Mean sample individual, modal dummy values	18.3	41.4	23.2
3. As 2 but age + 5	23.0	46.2	29.6
4. As 2 but 3 years more within industry experience.	26.6	61.1	33.4
5. As 2 but a 20% higher business failure rate	14.6	30.8	19.4
6. As 2 but in agricultural sector	61.6	155.4	68.7
7. As 2 but started while unemployed	12.7	22.7	22.1
8. As 2 but 5 years more general labour experience	14.4	45.8	13.6

Note: The results in the second column, *compulsory exits*, are obtained by treating voluntary exits as right-censored observations. The results in the third column, *voluntary exits*, are obtained likewise: by treating compulsory exits as right-censored observations.

in the third column. The more general labour experience, the more easily self-employment is ended by means of voluntary exit (probably due to better outside options) rather than business failure.

Conclusion

The objective of this study has been to find and to quantify individual-specific empirical determinants of self-employment duration and entrepreneurial success. I estimated both a single-risk and a competing-risks model on a sample of young white male self-employed in the United States (from the NLSY79). All conclusions can at most be generalized to this group. The (statistically) distinct exit destinations are compulsory and voluntary exits out of self-employment.

The selection of regressors to explain business duration, that is, the single-risk model, has largely been based on the empirical evidence pertaining to related types of studies, because of the lack of a theoretical model of person-oriented determinants of self-employment duration. I have developed a simple statistical relationship between regressor effects in the more frequently performed stock and entry studies on the one hand and regressor effects in a duration model on the other. Another class of empirical studies that gives some insight into duration determinants is that of self-employment exit studies. Of course, the evidence collected on self-employment duration has also been taken into consideration while searching for potential determinants in this study. I basically derive the explanatory variables for the hazard for compulsory exits (that is, business failures in the competing-risks model) in the competing-risks model from classical theories of business success and failure by economists such as Say, Marshall, Schumpeter and Knight.

The estimation results of the single-risk model are more or less consistent with the hypotheses derived from these other classes of self-employment studies. The business hazard varies with age, within-industry and within-occupation experience and not with the other usual human capital determinants of wages such as education and general labour market experience. And the most important individual determinants of entry into self-employment, years of self-employment experience and assets (see Chapter 3), play no significant role for self-employment duration. However, the motivation and enthusiasm with which a business venture is started influences its estimated duration significantly.

While one's individual (un)employment situation at the start of a venture affects its length significantly, the regional unemployment rate is of no importance at all for the hazard rate. Entry, on the contrary, appeared to react to these macro and micro measures of unemployment the other way around (Chapter 3). Hence, the important relationship between self-employment and unemployment depends on whether a macro or micro indicator of the latter is selected. The business failure rate, a straight measure of business conditions, is a highly significant determinant of the duration of an individual's business venture. The hazard for exit out of business ownership is an increasing function of calendar time up until 27 months and then decreases.

The results of the competing-risks model, which distinguishes compulsory from voluntary exits, could be useful for initiating policy measures aiming at longer-lasting business ventures. The model shows in which cases business hazards are high through a lack of motivation to continue and in which cases compulsory exits should be prevented. Policy recommendations are discussed in Chapter 9.

Notes

*   *Small Business Economics*, **21**(1), 2003, 1–17, 'Business survival and success of young small business owners: an empirical analysis', C.M. van Praag, © 2003. Reprinted with kind permission of Springer Science and Business Media.
1.   See Ridder (1987) for a similar formulation.
2.   References to the empirical sources of each sign as well as explanations about the various sample characteristics and variable definitions can be found in van Praag (1996). Empirical findings for several countries, years and subgroups and with various definitions for regressor variables have been brought together. Variables without any significant effects are omitted. Furthermore, Table 6.2 does not include variables, which have

previously been included only in 'inflow' studies. Inflow studies by themselves do not generate relevant predictions.

3. I know that no other transition has taken place within any month due to the manual way of obtaining these durations. Therefore, observations are complete and a continuous model in months is appropriate.

4. Note that entries are observed over the entire period; the sample is not a cohort.

5. The result reported is for self-employment experience in years. Replacing this with a 'mere self-employment experience' dummy does not alter this result.

6. See Meager (1992) for a discussion on the relationship between unemployment and self-employment. I have the advantage of the availability of both a personal and a macro measure of unemployment.

7. Furthermore, I know that it is usually believed that farmer-entrepreneurs are so different from others that they should be analysed separately. However, a dummy referring to the occupation 'farmer' was insignificant, as were all dummies referring to occupations. Farmers are included in this particular analysis because we have no reason to exclude them. Moreover, fewer than 10 per cent of the entrepreneurs are active in the agricultural business, and only 2.5 per cent of the total number of entrepreneurs is active in the occupation 'farmer'. It will be no surprise with such a small fraction of farmers that the results found are not significantly altered when the group of farmers is excluded from the analysis.

8. Provided that the NLSY79 variables matched to these historical success indicators represent the same ideas.

9. The test that renders this result can be described as follows. The absolute value of the log likelihood of the competing-risks model is 602. This value is compared to the log likelihood of the single-risk model. However, the single-risk model is not nested in the competing-risks model. I therefore apply the likelihood ratio test as presented in Lindeboom and Theeuwes (1991), designed especially for this purpose. It tests the null hypothesis that $\theta_o(t) = \theta_w(t) = 1/2[\theta(t)]$. The value of the likelihood ratio test statistic is 36, implying that the hazards for compulsory and voluntary transitions are statistically distinct.

10. The predicted durations do not depend on the amount of time passed. I insert average values for the time-varying variables. These values are averaged over the (calendar) period in business and also over persons.

PART IV

ENTREPRENEURSHIP SUCCESS/VENTURE PERFORMANCE: HUMAN AND FINANCIAL CAPITAL

7   Human capital

Introduction
To stimulate the further development of entrepreneurs, policy makers have, for instance, implemented entrepreneurship stimulation programmes in schools, and have made several subsidies and support services available for start-ups and small firms. However, the question remains in which way optimal stimulation of entrepreneurial performance can be achieved. There is one factor that both academic scholars and policy makers see as an important determinant of entrepreneurial performance, namely human capital. It is the topic of this chapter.

The correct measurement of the magnitude of the returns to human capital is therefore of the utmost importance to devise and implement effective policies. However, a recent meta-analysis (van der Sluis et al., 2003) reveals that the effect of formal schooling, one of the most prominent manifestations of human capital, on entrepreneurial performance has not yet been measured consistently. This is due to shortcomings in the empirical strategies applied so far. Previous studies measuring the relationship between education and entrepreneurial performance merely measure (conditional) correlations rather than causal effects. No attempt has yet been made to apply identification strategies such as instrumental variables (IV), twins studies and the like in order to estimate causal effects that are not biased due to the neglect of unobserved heterogeneity and the endogenous nature of the decision to invest in schooling.

My aim is to measure the returns to education (RTE) for entrepreneurs and relate its magnitude to the RTE for employees. To this end, I shall estimate the RTE for both entrepreneurs and employees. Using the same methodology for both groups of labour market participants will allow a comparison of the size of the omitted ability biases, the magnitude of the RTE, and the importance of sample selection for both groups. Thus, the performance measure of labour market success used for entrepreneurs as well as employees is earnings. To investigate the effects of omitted ability and endogenous education, I include a set of detailed ability proxies into the regression equations that are estimated by means of a random-effects model applying an IV approach. As in the application in Chapters 3 and 6, estimation is based on a sample from the US National Longitudinal Survey of Youth cohort (NLSY).

The results from this study reveal that the RTE are higher for entrepreneurs than for employees, and that applying an IV approach widens the difference between the two. The rather large difference cannot be attributed to sample selection or any of the other alternative explanations I address when performing robustness checks. I therefore arrive at interesting policy recommendations that follow from the estimation results under quite broad assumptions. These are included in Chapter 9.

This chapter is organized in the following way. The next section provides some theoretical developments pertaining to the relationship between education and successful entrepreneurship. The third section presents an overview of the empirical literature of the RTE for entrepreneurs. It also describes the methods used for obtaining unbiased estimates of the RTE for employees. The fourth section describes the sample used and the methodology applied. In the fifth section, the estimation results are presented for both entrepreneurs and employees, using the same variables and the same estimation techniques. Moreover, several robustness checks are discussed briefly. In the final section, results are discussed and conclusions are provided.

Theory

Human capital theory in general indicates that previous knowledge plays a critical role in intellectual performance; it assists in the integration and accumulation of new knowledge as well as the adaptation to new situations (Weick, 1996). Knowledge may be defined as either tacit ('know-how') or explicit ('know what') (Davidsson and Honig, 2003).

Individuals may increase their knowledge through formal education while informal education is gained through work or 'life' experience. Indeed, the main factors affecting earnings are education and experience in the Mincerian specification (see Mincer, 1974). Although tests of human capital theory have mostly been performed on employees, there is no reason to believe that the same relationship would not hold for the entrepreneurial sector of the labour market. Marshall was already a proponent of the thesis that human capital is closely associated with successful entrepreneurship (see Marshall, [1890] 1930 and Chapter 2). As Davidsson and Honig (2003) assert, making entrepreneurial decisions about complex problems utilizes an interaction of tacit and explicit knowledge.

Human capital is not only acknowledged for its productive effect on the quality or quantity of labour supplied, it also has value as a signal of productive ability in labour markets without complete information (Spence, 1973; Wolpin, 1977; Riley, 2002).[1] Like the empirical validity of human capital theory, the empirical validity of the screening value of education has also largely been assessed on the employees' subsample of the labour market. The question is, whether the signalling effect, on top of a productive effect of education, is as likely for entrepreneurs as for employees.

Many of the empirical tests devised to quantify the signalling effect of education for employees (Wolpin, 1977) assume that entrepreneurs, not having a prospective employer, can be treated as an unscreened control group. An empirical test in support of the screening hypothesis would therefore demonstrate that entrepreneurs have a smaller positive return to schooling than employees. I question the assumption that such a signal would be useless for entrepreneurs for two reasons. First, when acquiring education, the future entrepreneur might intend to work for an employer first. Second, there might be substantial screening from prospective capital suppliers, customers and other stakeholders. Education might then be used as a signal. The RTE could thus be of similar levels for employees and entrepreneurs. A comparison of these returns is therefore an empirical matter.

Empirical evidence
The relationship between schooling and entrepreneurship (entry and) performance has been measured in various empirical studies. Van der Sluis et al. (2003) provide an overview of such empirical studies into the impact of schooling on entrepreneurship selection and performance. In that study, an extensive meta-analysis is performed to assess whether there are any consistent findings from the empirical literature about the impact of education on entrepreneurship in industrialized countries.[2] To what extent are performance and education related? And, is the beneficial effect of education on performance stronger or weaker for entrepreneurs than for employees?

Four important outcomes result from this meta-analysis. First, the impact of schooling on performance is significantly positive for 67 per cent of the observations. We conclude that entrepreneurship performance is significantly affected by schooling.

Second, the meta-analysis gives insight into the level of the RTE for entrepreneurs. This insight, though, can be based on only a small subsample of US observations that uses similar measures for education and earnings. The return to a marginal year of schooling in terms of the income it generates is 6.1 per cent on average. This means that each additional year of education, on average, increases an individual's (annual) earnings by 6.1 per cent.

Third, the meta-analysis allows a comparison of the rate of return to education for entrepreneurs to the returns for employees. This comparison is based on the results from the 20 studies in the literature that compare the two groups of labour market participants using one data set and thereby one set of definitions, time period, country and the like. From these studies, the third result is obtained: the RTE are at least as high for employees as for entrepreneurs. More specifically, all studies pertaining to Europe indicate that the RTE are slightly lower for entrepreneurs than for employees. However, the opposite result is found for the studies that pertain to the United States, where the RTE are slightly higher for entrepreneurs. The differences between the two groups, in both Europe and the United States, are very small and insignificant.

The fourth conclusion from the meta-analysis is striking: all results obtained so far are potentially biased. Estimation and identification strategies used to identify the effect of education on performance have merely measured the (conditional) correlation between education and performance rather than the causal effect, the estimate of interest.

There are at least two possible sources of inconsistency when OLS, the most common estimation procedure, is used to estimate this relationship. First, the schooling decision is probably endogenous in a performance equation because individuals are likely to base their schooling investment decision, at least in part, on the expected payoffs to their investment. Second, there may be unobserved individual characteristics, such as ability and motivation, that affect both the schooling level attained and subsequent business performance. The omission of these unobserved characteristics from a performance equation would also serve to bias OLS estimates. Several methods to cope with these problems have been applied recently to estimate the RTE for employees. The general conclusion is that OLS estimates of the RTE for employees are biased downwards (Ashenfelter et al., 1999).

The potential bias also raises suspicion about the comparisons of RTEs for entrepreneurs and employees. The neglect of unobserved influential characteristics and not dealing with the endogenous nature of the education decision can have a different impact on the estimate of the RTE for entrepreneurs and employees (see Griliches, 1977). As a result, the conclusions from such comparisons should be re-evaluated.

The last conclusion from the meta-analysis, that is, that the causal and distinct effect of education on entrepreneur performance has not yet been measured properly, puts all other conclusions in a different perspective. The remainder of this section is devoted to a short presentation of possible methods of obtaining more consistent estimates and to the discussion of a recent application of one of these methods. This will be followed by a re-evaluation of the conclusions from the meta-analysis.

Estimation strategies for measuring the effect of education on outcomes
There are basically four methods to account for the potential problems of endogeneity and/or unobserved heterogeneity when estimating the RTE. All four have been applied to the estimation of the RTE for *employees* (Ashenfelter et al., 1999).

The first strategy for coping with unobserved ability is to try to make the unobservable observable. Various proxies of intelligence and test scores have been added to equations from which estimates of RTE result. The effects so far of adding ability controls on the estimated RTE are ambiguous (see ibid., Table 3).

The second strategy to identify causal effects is setting up a randomized experiment. This approach has not yet been much applied in labour economics research (Leuven et al., 2003). The proper design of an experiment requires a random assignment of individuals into a treatment group (participating in schooling) and a control group (not participating in schooling). In this manner, the choice to follow education is forced. The problem is that setting up an experiment where some people do not get (higher) education but others do, is often ethically not feasible.

The third strategy uses the variation in schooling, and income between monozygotic twins to estimate RTE. This approach has been used to identify employees' RTE (for example, Ashenfelter and Krueger, 1994; Behrman and Rosenzweig, 1999; Rouse, 1999, and Bonjour et al., 2003). The basic idea is that monozygotic twins share identical genetic endowment and usually experience even more similar environments than non-twin siblings. It seems then that comparing monozygotic twins should control thoroughly for otherwise unobserved heterogeneity. In general, these studies render a higher estimate of the RTE of employees than OLS (Ashenfelter et al., 1999).

The fourth strategy identifies causal effects using an IV approach. The idea is to imitate a field experiment where economic characteristics are randomly allocated among individuals to estimate their effects. This strategy therefore enables the unbiased measurement of the effect of, for instance, schooling, assuming a random allocation of schooling levels among individuals, independent of their expected payoffs or relevant unobserved background variables. With IV, problems relate to the availability and quality of identifying variables (Angrist and Krueger, 1991). In general, IV estimates of the returns to an employee's education are higher than OLS estimates (Ashenfelter et al., 1999). In the following, I shall discuss an application of the IV identification strategy.

Application: RTE for entrepreneurs and employees in the United States
Van der Sluis et al. (2004) compare the magnitude of the RTE for entrepreneurs and employees. Hence, the performance measure used in this study for both entrepreneurs and employees is earnings. Using the same methodology for both samples, a random effects model using IV was estimated, while including a set of detailed ability proxies.

Data and methodology
We use a sample drawn from the US NLSY79.[3] We replicate several aspects of an earlier study, that is, Blackburn and Neumark (1993; BN hereafter) which estimated the RTE for employees based on the same sample. The sample from the NLSY79 is a rich panel consisting of more than 6000 individuals and 19 annual earnings.[4] From these 6111 persons we extracted, per year observed, the hourly wage, the total years of education completed and various exogenous variables.

A particularly relevant background variable included in the NLSY79 is the 'Armed Services Vocational Aptitude Battery' (ASVAB), which is an IQ-like test score. The test score was administered in 1979–80, that is, before most educational and labour choices had been made, and can therefore be treated as exogenous. It is included in the income equations for both entrepreneurs and employees. In this manner the difference between the RTE resulting from using merely OLS with and without such controls can be compared.[5]

A second important feature of the NLSY79 is the presence of detailed family background variables. These variables were administered in 1979–80, but their recollected values pertain mostly to the respondents' family backgrounds at the age of 14. Consistent with BN, we use some of these variables as identifying instruments for the respondent's education. These family background characteristics are possibly good predictors of the educational level of the respondent while otherwise independent of their future wage.

A third relevant feature of the sample is that it includes both entrepreneurs and employees, and records individuals' switches between these states over time. All entrepreneurship spells, also short ones, are recorded. Therefore, the subsample of entrepreneurs does not suffer from survival bias, that is, the RTE will not pertain to surviving entrepreneurs only. Moreover, the incomes and all other relevant variables are measured in a comparable way for both groups such that the RTE for employees and entrepreneurs can be estimated in a comparable fashion.

A fourth important feature of the NLSY79 is its panel character. Nineteen years of information on approximately 6000 individuals results in a large number of data points. The panel character of the NLSY79 is exploited to correct for cohort effects, age effects and macroeconomic shocks.[6]

Estimation results
The estimation results for the effect of education on income for both entrepreneurs and employees are reported in Table 7.1. The left half of the table pertains to entrepreneurs, the right to employees.

Table 7.1   Determinants of income for entrepreneurs and employees (1979–2000)

Log hourly earnings	Entrepreneurs						Employees					
	OLS (1)		OLS (2)		RE IV (3)		OLS (4)		OLS (5)		RE IV (6)	
	Coef.	(|t|)	Coef.	(|t|)	Coef.	(|t|)	Coef.	(|t|)	Coef.	(|t|)	Coef.	(|t|)
Years of education	0.071	(7.9)***	0.067	(6.7)***	0.142	(5.5)***	0.067	(33.5)***	0.059	(29.5)***	0.107	(15.3)***
Academic score			0.026	(0.4)	−0.142	(1.6)			0.015	(1.2)	−0.093	(4.2)***
Non-academic score			−0.002	(0.0)	0.075	(1.0)			0.064	(4.9)***	0.113	(6.6)***
Male	0.668	(15.2)***	0.668	(14.8)***	0.648	(13.0)***	0.242	(26.9)***	0.229	(26.9)***	0.240	(24.0)***
Married	0.025	(0.8)	0.025	(0.8)	0.026	(0.7)	0.058	(14.5)***	0.058	(14.5)***	0.058	(14.5)***
Hispanic	−0.123	(1.1)	−0.113	(1.0)	−0.094	(0.7)	−0.005	(0.2)	0.014	(0.6)	0.018	(0.7)
Black	−0.244	(2.8)***	−0.231	(2.6)***	−0.235	(2.1)**	−0.136*	(9.7)***	−0.090	(6.0)***	−0.103	(5.7)***
Constant	−0.962	(1.1)	−0.926	(1.1)	−1.59	(1.8)*	0.048	(0.5)	0.145	(1.6)	−0.499	(3.8)***
R^2 within	0.18		0.18		0.19		0.52		0.52		0.53	
R^2 between	0.33		0.33		0.32		0.47		0.48		0.43	
R^2 overall	0.28		0.28		0.27		0.49		0.50		0.47	
N	3519		3519		2952		55769		55769		47152	

Note: Each estimation controls for year effects, age effects and macroeconomic shocks (Deaton, 2000). Other control variables included and not reported are 'locus-of-control beliefs', health status, regions, and levels of urbanization (SMSA). Coefficients are significant at the 1% level if the corresponding absolute *t*-value is at least 2.58 (marked with ***), at the 5% level if the corresponding absolute *t*-value is at least 1.96 (marked with **). They are marginally significant (at the 10% level) if the corresponding *t*-value is at least 1.65 (marked with *).

The results in the first and fourth columns show that the OLS estimate of the RTE is 7.1 per cent for entrepreneurs and 6.7 per cent for employees. In accordance with previous studies using US data, the returns are slightly higher for entrepreneurs than for employees, though of the same order of magnitude (Fredland and Little, 1981; Tucker, 1985, 1987; Evans and Leighton, 1990; Robinson and Sexton, 1994).

Next, as a first step to increasing the quality of these estimates, we control for potential bias due to omitted ability by including the academic and non-academic ability proxies from the ASVAB test scores. Columns two and five show that the estimates for RTE drop for both entrepreneurs and employees to 6.7 and 5.9 per cent, respectively. All other results remain approximately the same. These results indicate that the RTEs are biased upward when ability is omitted, consistent with Ashenfelter et al. (1999).[7]

Of course, there are many reasons why years of schooling could be correlated with the disturbance term, and one of these is unobserved ability. In addition, inclusion of IQ scores does not completely purge the estimated returns from ability bias (IQ scores are only proxies and neither academic nor non-academic ability is necessarily perfectly correlated with on-the-job ability); nor is it sufficient to control for endogeneity since ability is not necessarily perfectly correlated with time-discounting behaviour and/or with risk aversion and other such factors. Therefore, applying the IV procedure next is relevant.

The third (and sixth) columns show the (second-stage) estimation results when using an IV approach estimated by two-stage least squares (2SLS): applying IV results in significantly higher estimates of the RTE. The increase from 6.7 to 10.7 per cent for employees is comparable to increases resulting from applying IV instead of OLS in previous applications, such as BN. A novel observation is the even greater jump in the estimates pertaining to entrepreneurs: the IV estimate is twice as high as the OLS estimate of 7.1 per cent and amounts to 14.2 per cent. This leads to a remarkable result: in the United States, the RTE for entrepreneurs are estimated to be much higher than for employees. Previous research based on OLS estimates resulted in much smaller and insignificant differences.

However, before I take this novel result at face value, I first extend the quality and validity of the instruments chosen and the relevance of taking account of the endogenous character of schooling at all. I then discuss several robustness checks that we performed to see whether the RTE are really higher for entrepreneurs than for employees and to be able to interpret the result appropriately. These extensions are crucial for the assessment of the credibility of this result.

Choice of instruments

For the instrumentation of the possibly endogenous education variable we follow BN and use a set of background variables as identifying instruments. Although administered in 1979–80, these variables are usually recollections of household characteristics at the age of 14 (for example, the presence of a library card in the household). Following BN, we use those variables as identifying instruments that pass the criteria for quality and validity. The quality criterion comes down to requiring a sufficient correlation between the set of instruments and the endogenous regressor, education in this case. Instruments are valid if they affect performance via the education equation only. A set of instruments therefore passes the validity test if it is not correlated with the error term in the performance equation.

Variables proposed by BN as components of the set of identifying instruments were dropped if they turned out to be invalid. The resulting set of valid identifying instruments that is of sufficient quality differs only slightly between entrepreneurs and employees; it consists of 'A library card present in the household at age 14', 'Magazines present in the household at age 14', 'Father's education level', 'Mother's education level', 'A dummy for the presence of a male in the household', 'Number of siblings', 'Number of older siblings', 'Whether a foreign language is spoken in the household' and, finally, a dummy measuring 'Whether both parents are present in the household'. Appendix Table 7A.1 provides the estimation results of this first-stage regression, that is, where an individual's number of years of schooling is explained. It shows that for both entrepreneurs and employees the proposed set of determinants explains the variation among individuals in years of schooling attained quite satisfactorily: both R^2s are about 40 per cent.

However, critical evaluations of using family background as identifying instruments for education in an income equation have been expressed by Card (1999), who doubts the validity of instrument sets consisting of parental background variables. The idea is that family background variables are very likely to be correlated with a child's innate ability, and hence affect not only her or his educational attainment choices, but also expected returns from school. Such a set of instruments would therefore not be valid. We acknowledge this drawback of our choice of instruments. At the same time we try to measure and minimize its potential negative effects by performing Sargan's validity test (Davidson and MacKinnon, 1993) and by including indicators for the child's ability into the regression.

Indeed, the resulting set of identifying instruments for education passes the tests of quality and validity. We next perform a Hausman test (Hausman, 1978), which answers the question: 'Is schooling indeed endogenous in the income equations for entrepreneurs and employees?'.

The positive answer to this question resulting from the test supports the idea that treating years of education as an exogenous variable is not admissible econometrically for both segments of the labour market.

Robustness checks
So far, the implicit assumption has been maintained that individuals' choices for education do not affect their choice of employment status, that is, for entrepreneur or employee. However, if they do affect this choice, the result that the RTE are higher for entrepreneurs than for employees could be caused by selectivity bias. This could be the case if: (i) entrepreneurs are less highly educated and RTE are decreasing; (ii) entrepreneurs are more highly educated and RTE are increasing. Both combinations of findings could render the current finding, that the RTE for entrepreneurs are higher, misleading. Figure 7.1 illustrates this idea. The left-hand side shows the combination of decreasing RTE and lower-educated entrepreneurs than employees, whereas the right-hand side shows the case of increasing RTE in combination with higher-educated entrepreneurs than employees. Hence, to investigate the validity of such alternative explanations, we analyse: (i) the returns to scale of education; and (ii) whether entrepreneurs have higher or lower education levels than employees, on average.

We analyse the returns to scale of education in two alternative ways. First, we split the sample of both entrepreneurs and employees into two equal parts: one with higher than median education levels, and the rest. A comparison of the resulting (four) sets of estimates shows that, if anything,

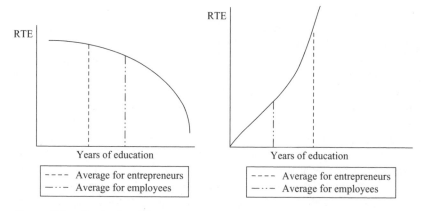

Figure 7.1   Example of how a non-constant RTE could lead to an alternative (selectivity-related) explanation for the finding that the RTE are higher for entrepreneurs

the RTE are increasing. Second, to check this result, we re-estimate the wage equations in Table 7.1 and include education squared as a determinant.[8] For the majority of entrepreneurs and employees the RTE turn out to be increasing in education. Selectivity would therefore only be a possible spurious explanation for the higher returns for entrepreneurs in the case where higher-educated individuals are selected for entrepreneurship, that is, as is the case in the left-hand side of Figure 7.1.

We use several methods to investigate the possibility that education determines the selection into self-employment positively. A first indication that selectivity is no issue is found by inspection of the mean education levels for entrepreneurs and employees: they are almost equal. Second, we find that the education level is not a significant determinant of the (time-varying) employment status when estimating a random effects probit model. A third test result pointing at no sample selection is obtained by applying a test by Nijman and Verbeek (1992), who suggest including a lag of the employment status in the wage regression.[9] The test results indicate that the lag is insignificant in the income equation of both entrepreneurs and employees. However, the disadvantage attached to including a lag of labour market experience gathered as an entrepreneur, is the possible productive effects of such indicators on income. We therefore include a lead instead of a lag of employment status into the wage equation and find the same result. The conclusion is consistent with previous findings: the meta-analysis (van der Sluis et al., 2003) demonstrated that 75 per cent of all studies find an insignificant effect of education on the selection of employment status. The overall conclusion is that self-selection is not a disturbing factor that would render our result pertaining to the comparison of the returns to education for entrepreneurs and employees invalid.

The second robustness check relates to the unit of measurement of the RTE. The estimations suggest that the percentage gain in income of an extra year of education is higher for entrepreneurs than for employees. The question is whether the RTE are also higher for entrepreneurs in absolute terms: 'Does a year of education generate more dollars per hour for an entrepreneur than for an employee?'. We answer this question by estimating RTEs using hourly pay as the dependent variable instead of log hourly pay, keeping all else equal. The results show that the RTE in dollars are also higher for entrepreneurs than for employees.

A third robustness check concerns the assumed log normality of the distribution of hourly pay. The estimates in Table 7.1 have been obtained under this assumption. Especially for entrepreneurs, this assumption might be questionable (Blanchflower and Meyer, 1994). Therefore, we recalculate (in a slightly less precise way) the percentage RTE for both groups without using the results obtained under the assumption of log normality of the hourly earnings distribution. The outcome again supports the claim that the returns are higher for entrepreneurs (with RTEs of, respectively, 14.1 and 12.7 per cent): the result is apparently invariant to the assumed distribution of earnings.

Our fourth robustness check relates to the question as to whether the difference in RTE between entrepreneurs and employees can be attributed to a *risk premium* obtained by higher-educated entrepreneurs. This would be a valid alternative explanation if more highly educated individuals require higher risk premia for being an entrepreneur. Higher-educated individuals might experience more additional income risk as an entrepreneur relative to an employee than would lower-educated individuals. The left-hand side of Figure 7.2 illustrates this risk-premium-related explanation.

However, we conclude that the risk-premium explanation is not valid, based on a combination of three observations derived from the data. The combined effect of these three observations is illustrated in the right-hand side of Figure 7.2. First, the (time-series) variance of the (unexplained parts of) entrepreneurial income is not higher for more highly educated individuals, all else equal. Second, the variance of an employee's income increases in the employee's education level. Third, the variance in earnings is lower for employees than for entrepreneurs, at all possible education levels. These three observations together imply that entrepreneurs are exposed to more income risk than employees are, but that the difference is a decreasing rather than an increasing function of education.

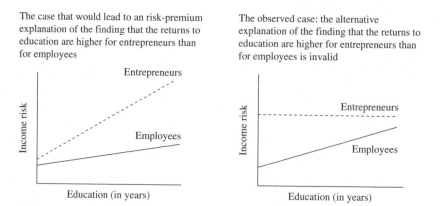

The case that would lead to an risk-premium explanation of the finding that the returns to education are higher for entrepreneurs than for employees

The observed case: the alternative explanation of the finding that the returns to education are higher for entrepreneurs than for employees is invalid

Figure 7.2   Example of how a non-constant income risk (in education) could explain higher RTE for entrepreneurs

Hence, the finding that the RTE are higher for entrepreneurs than for employees is not due to selectivity. It is due neither to wrong assumptions with regard to the functional form of the income distribution of entrepreneurs, nor to percentage gains that would not translate into absolute gains. Moreover, the higher RTE for entrepreneurs cannot be explained in terms of a higher risk premium for higher-educated entrepreneurs.

So why *is* education more valuable for entrepreneurs? We propose a simple explanation: entrepreneurs have more freedom to optimize their use of education. Entrepreneurs are not constrained by rules from superiors and can decide on how to put their education to its most productive use. In contrast, the organizational structure surrounding an employee makes it difficult to optimize the productive effect of education. Besides, the organization cannot adapt its structure to every individual due to organizational inertia and individual incompatibilities. This difference in ability to optimize the productivity of education for entrepreneurs and employees might therefore be an explanation for the higher RTE for entrepreneurs.

Discussion

A meta-analysis of the empirical evidence on the relationship between education and entrepreneurship performance, showed the following empirical regularities: (i) RTE are significantly positive for entrepreneurs; (ii) RTE are 6 per cent for entrepreneurs; (iii) RTE are of similar size for entrepreneurs and for employees; and (iv) the empirical evidence may have produced (probably downwards) biased results due to using estimation methods that fail to identify causal effects. The conclusions from the meta-analysis should therefore be re-evaluated based on novel findings from a recent application of the IV methodology that measures the RTE better.

We have performed this study and find that (US) entrepreneurs benefit more from an additional year of education than their employed counterparts and more than was suggested by previous results: the RTE are shown to be higher for entrepreneurs (14 and 10 per cent, respectively). As the difference in estimated returns is much smaller and insignificant when using the common estimation procedure OLS, I conclude that the bias resulting from not accounting for endogeneity is larger for entrepreneurs than for employees, but do not yet understand why this is so.

Based on these results, I re-evaluate the conclusions from the meta-analysis and conclude as follows: (i) the RTE for entrepreneurs are indeed positive and (ii) much higher than previous measures indicated: they seem to amount to 14 per cent in the United States, and (iii) are thereby much higher than the RTE for employees in the same country; (iv) previous (OLS) estimates were indeed biased.

However, care should be taken about drawing too strong conclusions yet. Replicating the study currently discussed with different data, also for various countries and possibly with different sets of instruments, would be useful to confirm the findings that are now based on one study only. Alternatively, these findings could be validated (or not) using different identification strategies, such as twins research. In any case, more insight into the causal relationship between education and the performance of entrepreneurs is required.

Parker and van Praag (2004) have recently made a step forward in this respect: they estimate the returns to education for Dutch entrepreneurs using a similar approach. They also find that the RTE are higher for entrepreneurs than the percentage gains from education that are usually found for Dutch employees.

Appendix 7A

Table 7A.1   *Estimation results from the first-stage education equation (OLS)*

Variable	Entrepreneurs		Employees	
	Estimate	($|t$-value$|$)	Estimate	($|t$-value$|$)
Dummy: library card			0.383	(5.89)***
Dummy: magazines	0.491	(3.30) ***		
Father's education	0.129	(5.61) ***	0.191	(21.22) ***
Mother's education	0.205	(6.41) ***		
Dummy: no male at home			0.484	(4.14) ***
Number of siblings	−0.128	(2.78) ***	−0.141	(7.42) ***
Number of older siblings	0.097	(1.98) **	0.086	(4.10) ***
Dummy: foreign language spoken	0.405	(1.91) *	0.198	(1.98) **
Dummy: both parents present	0.380	(2.50) **	0.665	(7.92) ***
Constant	4.646	(2.28) **	9.323	(39.50) ***
R^2	0.40		0.39	
Sample size, N	2951		47 040	

Note: Each estimation controls for year effects, age effects and macroeconomic shocks (Deaton 2000). Coefficients are significant at the 1% level if the corresponding absolute t-value is at least 2.58 (marked with ***), at the 5% level if the corresponding absolute t-value is at least 1.96 (marked with **). They are marginally significant (at the 10% level) if the corresponding t-value is at least 1.65 (marked with *).

Notes

1. In signalling, the party with private information – that is, the employee in the selection and hiring process by employers – takes the lead in adopting behaviour that, upon appropriate interpretation, reveals information about his type of productivity.
2. See van der Sluis et al. (2006) for a meta-analysis pertaining to less-developed countries.
3. This data set was also used in Chapters 3 and 6. However, in the current application we have a longer time series at our disposal, that is, to the year 2000.
4. I use more waves from NLSY79 in this study than in the studies documented in the preceeding chapters using the same data set (Chapters 3 and 6). The analysis underlying the studies discussed in Chapters 3 and 6 have been performed earlier when these more recent waves were not yet available.
5. Consistent with BN, we adapt the ASVAB (administered in 1979–80) test score in two respects. First, we separate the test score, which is composed of ten separate scores, into an 'academic' and a 'non-academic' component. Second, we remove the age effects from the ASVAB, as respondents are of different ages when the test is administered. We do so by regressing each normalized test score on a set of seven age dummies and we use the individuals' residuals as the new test scores.
6. To this end, we use a decomposition technique (Deaton, 2000), not used by BN, to rescale cohort and time trends such that they become orthogonal to each other.
7. Contrary to expectations, not all of the results for the ability proxies are significant, especially not for entrepreneurs. Using one composite measure of (both academic and non-academic) ability would generate positive coefficients for this ability measure in both equations, while leaving all other coefficients unchanged (see van der Sluis et al., 2004).
8. We account for the potential endogenous character of education squared by including the residuals of the first-stage education equation and the first-stage squared education equation.
9. The underlying assumption is that sample selection is related to idiosyncratic errors only.

8 Financial capital

Introduction
The observation of resource spending by governments for the sake of increasing the number of higher qualified entrepreneurs is explained not only by the social benefit pertaining to entrepreneurial endeavour, but also by the perceived existence of undesirable impediments to the supply of entrepreneurs. A lack of capital is one of these factors and is the focus of this chapter.

The objective of this chapter is to answer the questions: 'To what extent is the performance of a small business founder's entrepreneurial venture, once started, affected by capital constraints at the time of inception?', and, 'What happens to performance when an entrepreneur has insufficient capital to reach the optimal investment level or timing?'.

Financial capital constraints might prevent entrepreneurs from creating buffers against random shocks, thereby affecting the timing of investments negatively. Moreover, capital constraints might debar entrepreneurs from the pursuit of more capital-intensive strategies. Thus, what I am aiming at is measuring the effect of initial capital constraints on venture performance. Merely measuring the correlation between capital constraints and performance would not be sufficient, since it would (wrongly) include *spurious* factors that affect access to capital as well as performance directly, such as ability and motivation. The distinction between causal and spurious factors is crucial since policy implications diverge. In the first case, supplying more capital to entrepreneurs who are hindered from following the optimal investment scheme would improve performance. In the second case, it will not, because the capital constraint itself is not the binding restriction, but the factors underlying it.

Much (empirical) research effort has been put into measuring the effect of capital constraints on the *selection* of individuals for entrepreneurial positions.[1] The conclusion is that capital constraints bind: a significant proportion of individuals willing to enter the entrepreneurial population are hampered by a lack of sufficient capital. Capital markets are not market clearing for the segment of new firms (Fazzari et al., 1988). Personal savings and loans from friends and relatives is by far the largest source of capital in newly started firms (for example, Parker, 2004).

Research effort has also been devoted, though to a lesser extent, to measuring the correlation between access to capital and entrepreneurship *performance* once the stage of start-up has been successfully completed.[2] This chapter aims to contribute to this category of research.

This chapter is organized as follows. The next section gives some insight into the theoretical debate about the relationship between capital and entrepreneurship. The third section discusses the empirical evidence so far of the relationship between capital constraints and the performance of the entrepreneur. The fourth section describes a simple model set-up that should clarify the contribution of the study described in this chapter to the existing empirical literature. The fifth section describes the current empirical application. The final sections describe the data, the estimation results and the conclusions from the study.

Theory

There has been a lively theoretical debate about the relationship between access to capital and investment decisions of entrepreneurs. The first stream of thought assumes perfect capital markets. External funds provide a perfect substitute for internal capital in this full information case. An entrepreneur's financial conditions are irrelevant to investment: investment decisions are independent of whether one needs to 'pay' the opportunity cost of capital ownership, or the interest rate of borrowing money. Proponents of this view can be traced back to Richard Cantillon ([1755] 1979); see Chapter 2.

The second stream of research in entrepreneurship assumes less than perfect capital markets due to the existence of imperfect and asymmetric information. The latter makes it costly or impossible for providers of external finance to evaluate the quality of an entrepreneur's investment opportunities. This might debar (some) entrepreneurs from sufficient access to external capital, that is, type I credit rationing. The common theoretical explanation for credit rationing *vis-à-vis* newly founded firms is a severe lack of observable and verifiable information about the entrepreneur's type, his plans and the associated risks. The asymmetry of information about the entrepreneur's type and behaviour will potentially lead to agency problems: adverse selection and moral hazard (LeRoy and Singell, 1987; Boadway et al., 1998; De Meza and Webb, 2000). The foresight of these problems might prevent the start of ventures. This view has a history in economic thought, too. The performance of the entrepreneur in the classical and neoclassical theories of Say ([1803] 1971) and Marshall ([1890] 1930) is hindered by a lack of own capital since borrowed capital requires a reputation (Say) or a risk premium (Marshall); see Chapter 2.

The continuation of this debate in entrepreneurship research, starting in the late 1980s, was largely empirical. To prevent adverse selection in actual credit markets, the point of departure is not credit rationing in response to the hidden-type problem but 'redlining' instead. Redlining, screening or credit scoring (De Meza and Webb, 2000) involves capital suppliers using selection procedures based on a set of indicator variables for the expected performance of entrepreneurs and their projects. Those failing to score sufficiently highly on the criteria are denied credit. Thus, determinants of entrepreneurship performance such as education and experience might moreover turn out to be indicators of access to capital (Bates, 1990; Scherr et al., 1993). This clarifies part of the discussion below as to whether human (sometimes also social) capital variables have been included in the empirical models.

Empirical evidence: capital constraints and performance
To discriminate between the full and the asymmetric information case, several kinds of empirical research have been carried out. An overview is given in Table 8.1. The entries in the table show which studies have used a particular measure of capital constraints (columns) in combination with a particular performance measure (rows). The following subsections discuss each column of the table.

Relationship between assets and performance
Many researchers have related the size of family assets to the earnings (or job creation, growth or survival) of entrepreneurial ventures. Both Evans and Jovanovic (1989) and Cooper et al. (1994) find a positive association between assets and performance for US entrepreneurs. Taylor's (1999)

Table 8.1   Effect of financial capital on performance (empirical evidence from the literature)

Lack of access to capital measure Performance measure	Assets	Inheritance	Windfall gains
Earnings	EJ: +	HJR: +	
Survival	CGW: +; T: +; vP: 0; C: 0	HJR: +; BFN: +	LO: +
Growth	CGW: +; CTM: 0	BFN: +; CTM: +	CTM: +

Note: BFN: Burke, FitzRoy and Nolan (2002); CGW: Cooper, Gimeno-Gascon and Woo (1994); C: Cressy (1996); EJ: Evans and Jovanovic (1989); HJR: Holtz-Eakin, Joulfaian and Rosen (1994a); LO: Lindh and Ohlsson (1996); T: Taylor (1999); vP: van Praag (Chapter 6); CTM: Cowling, Taylor and Mitchell (2004). Bates (1990) is excluded from the literature overview because he has been unable to establish the conditional correlation of interest due to problems of multicollinearity.

result pertaining to the UK is supportive of Evans and Jovanovic and Cooper et al. The effect of a dummy indicating whether or not the respondent had received interest or dividend payments exceeding £100 is negative on the hazard and thus has a positive effect on survival. In Chapter 6, I also relate financial variables, that is, assets and a dummy for home ownership (frequently used as collateral), to survival of young entrepreneurs in the United States. The effect of these variables on the hazard of entrepreneurship is insignificant. Cressy's (1996) insignificant result on survival for the UK supports my findings in Chapter 6. Furthermore, Cowling et al. (2004) estimate that assets do not increase job creation by British entrepreneurs.

Several general disadvantages are attached to the studies in this category. First, the possibility of obtaining external finance remains unconsidered: it is assumed that the 'external route to obtain finance' is totally inaccessible. Second, a monotone relationship is assumed between assets and performance, while in reality it might well be the case that up to a certain point more access to capital might help in enhancing performance, but 'enough is enough'. This possible discontinuity in the relationship is not taken into account in the approach used in studies indicated in the first column of Table 8.2. A third drawback of the method in general is that 'family assets' is not an exogenous variable: without binding capital constraints, a correlation could still exist between assets and performance because of the entrepreneur's ability ('earning power') affecting both quantities. Finally, assets in general are badly reported in individual survey research and therefore the figures are unreliable, plagued with measurement error.

Relationship between inheritance receipt and performance
One of the major drawbacks of the approach of merely relating assets, as a measure of access to capital, to new venture performance is the possible endogenous character of assets. An interesting alternative might be the receipt of an inheritance: 'Studying the behavior of those who receive money is presumably as close as the economist can get to the idealized laboratory experiment in which some subjects are issued capital while those in a control group get none' (Blanchflower and Oswald, 1998, p. 28).

Holtz-Eakin et al. (1994a) were the first to estimate the relationship of this inheritance variable with firm *performance* rather than entry. They find a positive effect of receiving an inheritance on firm survival and earnings in the United States. Burke et al. (2002) estimate the effect of inheritance on both entry and performance where the latter is measured as survival and employment growth. They find all these relationships to be significantly positive. Cowling et al. (2004) find a positive effect of inheritance on job creation by entrepreneurs.

This innovative approach, however, solves only the third of the four drawbacks attached to the first approach. Indeed, if not applied adequately, an additional disadvantage is evoked by the inheritance approach:

> We find that young men's own financial assets exert a statistically significant but quantitatively modest effect on the transition to self-employment. In contrast, the capital of parents exerts a large influence. Parents' strongest effect runs, not through financial means, but rather through their own self-employment experience and business success. (Dunn and Holtz-Eakin, 2000, p. 282)[3]

Relationship between windfall gains and performance
Lindh and Ohlsson (1996) estimate the effect of windfall gains on the probability of *being* self-employed on a sample of Swedish individuals. They consider windfall gains as a dummy variable indicating whether people have ever won in lotteries or have ever received a personal or spousal inheritance. They find significant effects on self-employment of both inheritance and lottery prizes. However, upon inclusion of additional control variables (human capital) the significant effect of inheritance receipts vanishes whereas the effect of lottery prizes remains significant. This supports the finding by Dunn and Holtz-Eakin (2000) about the intergenerational correlation of entrepreneurship. The same holds for the findings by Cowling et al. (2004) that there is a positive effect of inheritance receipts on job creation, but they do not find such an effect of alternative indicators of windfall gains. Hence, their conclusion is also consistent with the explanation by Dunn and Holtz-Eakin (2000). The windfall gains approach, as ingenious as it is, does not solve the majority of the drawbacks associated with the first approach, though it somehow solves the problem of endogeneity.[4]

The following model set-up clarifies the first two drawbacks of the existing estimation methods: (i) the possibility of obtaining external finance remains unconsidered and (ii) a monotone relationship is assumed between assets and performance.

Model set-up
Consider the entrepreneurial performance measure gross receipts, as in Holtz-Eakin et al. (1994a) and consistent with Evans and Jovanovic (1989):

$$P_i = \theta_i f(k_i)\varepsilon, \tag{8.1}$$

where θ_i is individual i's entrepreneurial ability or business acumen, $f(\cdot)$ is a production function with one input, capital (k_i), and ε is a random factor to the production process.

Individuals know their ability, unlike the analyst or banker who observes an indicator function of ability, $\tilde{\theta}_i$ only. Ability varies across individuals. It is assumed that ε has mean 1 and finite variance and that $f(0) > 0$, that is, the firm can produce output even in the absence of any inputs, other than the entrepreneur's ability, as for example in the professional services industry.

A_i is defined as the value of the individual's personal assets; hence $A_i - k_i$ is generating capital income at rate r. The (risk-neutral) entrepreneur maximizes total income:

$$y_i = \theta_i f(k_i)\varepsilon + r(A_i - k_i). \tag{8.2}$$

The optimal investment level of capital into the entrepreneur's venture is therefore defined by:

$$\theta_i f'(k_i^*) = r. \tag{8.3}$$

I assume that A_i is a non-decreasing function of θ_i: entrepreneurial ability is an indicator for general 'earning power' from which assets might have resulted. The relationship between entrepreneurial ability and the amount of external capital required, at rate r, $k_i^* - A_i$, is therefore ambiguous.

Access by individual entrepreneurs to the most desirable amount of external capital, $l_i^* = k_i^* - A_i \geq 0$ at price r is constrained by the factor β_i, where $0 \leq \beta_i \leq 1$. $\beta_i = 1$ represents the fully constrained entrepreneur; $\beta_i = 0$ the unconstrained. The amount of external capital obtained is:

$$l_i = k_i - A_i = (1 - \beta_i)l_i^* = (1 - \beta_i)(k_i^* - A_i) \tag{8.4}$$

for all entrepreneurs. The value of β_i depends on 'borrowing power', which is dependent in turn on collateral and $\tilde{\theta}_i$.

The central question is to what extent β_i creates performance losses, that is, the effect of β_i on the expected (constrained) performance:

$$P_i = \theta_i f[k_i^* - \beta_i(k_i^* - A_i)] = \theta_i f[A_i + (1 - \beta_i)(k_i^* - A_i)]. \tag{8.5}$$

In order to get rid of the intruding effect of ability on the relationship between absolute performance and capital constraints, I consider relative performance:

$$\log P_i = \log \theta_i + \log f[k_i^* - \beta_i(k_i^* - A_i)]. \tag{8.6}$$

Equations (8.5) and (8.6) immediately show a drawback of all approaches as discussed in the previous subsection: simply looking at how a change in A_i affects performance does not measure the effect of capital constraints on performance.

In the following section, I discuss a recent study by van Praag et al. (2003), in which an attempt is made to measure the effect of capital constraints on performance while limiting as much as possible the biases resulting from the drawbacks that are attached to previous measurements.[5]

Application: capital constraints and the performance of entrepreneurs
We evaluate the effect of capital constraints on entrepreneurial performance on a panel of 1000 Dutch entrepreneurs. We use a direct individual indicator variable for initial capital constraints, unlike in previous research.

Measurement issues
The empirical proxy of the centrepiece of the analysis, β_i, is a dummy variable formed by the answer to the question: 'Did you experience problems in obtaining sufficient (external) capital at the start of your venture?'. The frequency of the three possible answers in the sample is given below.

Yes, and I didn't solve the problem	7%
Yes, but I solved the problem	17%
No	76%

The 7 per cent of entrepreneurs who experienced these problems but did not solve them are considered to be capital constrained, that is, $\beta_i = 1$. The other 93 per cent are characterized by $\beta_i = 0$: these entrepreneurs operate their businesses at the optimal level, k_i^*.[6]

In this manner, we cope with the first two drawbacks attached to all previously applied approaches: first, our estimate of β's coefficient measures the effect on performance of being capital constrained for the group of entrepreneurs who are indeed capital constrained. Other approaches generate an estimate of the mere effect of an increase in assets on performance. Second, our estimate of β's coefficient embodies the effect of capital constraints that remain after the possibility of obtaining external finance has been explored. Other approaches assume that external finance is totally inaccessible. Moreover, the fourth drawback, the issue that empirical measures of assets are plagued with measurement error, is also circumvented by not using such a measure. However, circumventing this measurement problem comes at a cost: we rely on self-reported subjective answers about capital constraints. Structural over- or under-reporting of this variable would lead to biased results.

Another limitation of our approach is that it does not solve the endogeneity issue, that is, the third drawback, although we try minimizing the bias in our estimates of $\partial P_i/\partial \beta_i$ by controlling as much as possible for ability and motivation. In what follows I describe how we deal with two sorts of potential bias.

First, $\partial P_i/\partial \beta_i$ might be biased upwards, due to redlining by capital suppliers based on $\tilde{\theta}_i$. This $\tilde{\theta}_i$ also has a direct (positive) impact on performance, thereby generating the bias. In our performance equations we control for human capital variables, $\tilde{\theta}_i^{HC}$ and for social capital variables, $\tilde{\theta}_i^{SC}$, that are known to affect entrepreneurship performance. The vector of human capital variables has the following elements: age, various sorts of general and specific work experience, and education.[7] The vector of social capital variables, $\tilde{\theta}_i^{SC}$, includes a dummy variable indicating the business owner's activity in an entrepreneur's network in the first year of operation. A(n emotionally supportive) partner is also considered potentially valuable social capital.[8] Furthermore, the vector includes proxies for the rate at which respondents used four major strategies of information gathering (revealed from factor analysis),[9] that is, focus on: (i) the branch; (ii) direct business relations; (iii) commercial relations; and (iv) fellow entrepreneurs.[10]

We furthermore include a vector of signals of entrepreneurial ability, θ_i, based on the known result of credit scoring by external capital suppliers: we consider the assignment of a loan by family/friends, banks, and in particular by business partners as informative about unobserved heterogeneity.

Second, $\partial P_i/\partial \beta_i$ might be biased downwards, due to:[11]

1. *Time hypothesis* People spending much time on other paid activities will probably show weaker venture performance and simultaneously face lower capital constraints. Without any additional corrective measures, this spurious effect would be included in an estimate of the coefficient for β_i leading to a downward bias. We therefore include a dummy variable that is 1 for entrepreneurs who spend more than 20 hours per week on other paid activities.

2. *Motivation hypothesis* Financial independence from the venture might be a cause for lower capital constraints and might simultaneously result in a weaker motivation. Without correction, this spurious effect would again lead to a downward bias. Two variables are included in the analysis to correct for this bias: (i) a categorized variable 'amount of other income available', and (ii) a dummy variable indicating financial dependence on the venture income.

Data

The panel results were derived from annual questionnaires conducted on a sample taken from all newly registered firms in the first quarter of 1994 with the Dutch Chamber of Commerce; some 1323 firm founders answered all subsequent annual questionnaires of 1995–97.[12] The information from the 1994 questionnaire was used for the construction of potential determinants of performance. Entrepreneurial performance itself, measured by (the logarithm of) profits and survival duration is measured exclusively by means of variables constructed from the subsequent questionnaires.[13] Thus, problems of serially reversed causality are prevented.

Estimation results

The first column of Table 8.2 shows the result from the Tobit estimation with (log) profit as the dependent variable and the capital constraint and some standard control variables as the only independent variables. The estimation result is consistent with binding capital constraints: entrepreneurs who suffer from a lack of capital for their initial business investments have 63 per cent lower profits. As was expected, column II in Table 8.2 shows that the effect of capital constraints on profit diminishes (to 59 per cent) when controlling for human capital effects, the capital constraint still being signifficant. Human capital, as was assumed, appears to simultaneously affect performance positively and the capital constraint itself negatively. The main factors of influence are various sorts of experience and education.

Controlling for social capital factors (column III) also has a diminishing effect on the capital constraint: the coefficient decreases further from 59 to 52 per cent and remains significant. The most important social capital factor is a spouse's emotional support. Other social capital factors of influence are the exploitation of commercial contacts and contacts with fellow entrepreneurs.

Our third hypothesis, that the capital constraint diminishes when correcting for financial screening factors, is not validated in this exercise (column IV). The capital constraint decreases from 52 to 51 per cent only, and remains significant. Moreover, financial screening factors have no additional significant effect on profits, suggesting that these factors do not reveal any heterogeneity in addition to human and social capital.

The addition of the next two blocks of variables (columns V and VI) serves to correct for the potential downward bias in the estimate for the capital constraint due to time and motivational constraints. It appears that the inclusion of indicators for time and motivational constraints does not, contrary to expectations, increase the absolute value of the coefficient pertaining to the capital constraint. The remaining as 'unbiased' as possible effect of the capital constraint on profit is a disadvantageous 51 per cent.

Table 8.2 Estimation results: capital constraints and profits

Profit	I	II	III	IV	V	VI
Capital constraint	−0.63 **	−0.59 **	−0.52 **	−0.51 **	−0.49 **	−0.51 **
Human capital						
Experience in business ownership		0.50 **	0.50 **	0.49 **	0.54 **	0.54 **
Experience relevant to business ownership		0.12	0.12	0.12	0.13	0.12
Experience in industry		0.71 **	0.67 **	0.67 **	0.66 **	0.65 **
Age divided by 10		0.30	0.11	0.14	0.11	0.05
Age divided by 10, then squared		−0.03	−0.01	−0.01	−0.01	0.00
High education		0.20*	0.19*	0.18	0.20 *	0.22 **
Experience as an employee		0.39*	0.36*	0.35*	0.41**	0.40 *
Social capital						
Contact with entrepreneurs in networks			−0.08	−0.08	−0.10	−0.10
Way of information gathering						
General channels			0.04	0.04	0.04	0.04
Direct business relations			0.05	0.05	0.06	0.06
Commercial relations			0.10 **	0.10 **	0.10 **	0.09 *
Fellow entre-preneurs			0.11 **	0.11 **	0.11 **	0.10 **
Emotional support from spouse			0.51 **	0.52 **	0.49 **	0.49 **
Presence of spouse			−0.21	−0.21	−0.17	−0.11

Table 8.2   (Continued)

Profit	I	II	III	IV	V	VI
Financial screening						
Share own capital in start capital				0.00	0.03	0.04
Fin. also by loanfrom family				0.00	−0.02	−0.02
Fin. also by bank				−0.01	0.00	−0.01
Fin. also by business partner(s)				0.23	0.24	0.25
Time constraint						
Spent 20+ hours on other paid activities					−0.35 **	−0.30 **
Motivation						
Other income available						−0.01
Dependent on profits from business						0.19
Constant	−2.06 **	−3.39 **	−3.07 **	−3.16 **	−2.97 **	−2.81 **
Sample size	1168	1168	1168	1168	1168	1168
Log likelihood	−1643	−1611	−1599	−1598	−1595	−1593

Note: Control variables included are 'gender', organizational structure, hours worked at the start and some start-up motives. *p-values ≤ 0.10; **p-value ≤ 0.05. t-values are not shown.

Table 8.3 shows determinants of duration. The effect of the capital constraint is in the same order of magnitude as in the profit equation: ranging from 63 per cent without corrections to 48 per cent with them. Column II shows that the inclusion of human capital factors diminishes the effect by 10 percentage points, whereas column III shows that social capital factors account for a decrease of another 6 percentage points. The other corrections have no significant effect. The remaining as 'unbiased' as possible effect of the capital constraint on duration is a disadvantageous 48 per cent.

When comparing the results tabulated in Tables 8.2 and 8.3, several patterns emerge. Entrepreneurs who acknowledge unsolvable initial capital

Table 8.3   Estimation results: capital constraints and duration

Duration	I	II	III	IV	V	VI
Capital constraint	−0.63**	−0.53*	−0.47*	−0.47 *	−0.47 *	−0.48*
Human capital						
Experience in business ownership		0.17	0.17	0.17	0.19	0.19
Experience relevant to business ownership		0.38**	0.29	0.29	0.30	0.30
Experience in industry		0.58**	0.53**	0.54 **	0.53 **	0.52**
Age divided by 10		0.68	0.77	0.77	0.77	0.75
Age divided by 10, then squared		−0.05	−0.07	−0.07	−0.07	−0.06
High education		−0.01	−0.08	−0.09	−0.08	−0.08
Experience as an employee		0.51*	0.43	0.44	0.45	0.45
Social capital						
Contact with entrepreneurs in networks			0.10	0.09	0.09	0.09
Way of information gathering:						
General channels			0.29**	0.29 **	0.29 **	0.29**
Direct business relations			−0.08	−0.08	−0.08	−0.08
Commercial relations			0.09	0.09	0.09	0.09
Fellow entrepreneurs			0.07	0.07	0.07	0.07
Emotional support from spouse			0.40	0.40	0.40	0.40
Presence of spouse			−0.47	−0.47	−0.46	−0.43
Financial screening						
Share own capital in start capital				0.05	0.05	0.07
Fin. also by loan from family				0.07	0.06	0.07
Fin. also by bank				−0.01	−0.01	−0.02
Fin. also by business partner(s)				0.01	0.01	0.02
Time constraint						
Spent 20+ hours on other paid activities					−0.07	−0.05

Table 8.3   (Continued)

Duration	I	II	III	IV	V	VI
Motivation						
Other income available						−0.01
Dependent on profits from business						0.07
Constant	3.29**	0.81	0.75	0.71	0.73	0.80
Sample size	1073	1073	1073	1073	1073	1073
Log likelihood	−1303	−1285	−1275	−1275	−1275	−1275

Note: Control variables included are 'gender', organizational structure, hours worked at the start and some start-up motives. *p-values $\leqslant 0.10$; **p-value $\leqslant 0.05$. t-values are not shown.

constraints experience lower profits, conditional upon survival, whereas their survival rate compares unfavourably with those who are not capital constrained. The size of the effect of capital constraints decreases when correcting for human and social capital factors, but it remains significant and relatively large. Financial screening, time and motivational constraints do not consistently show the expected effects, either directly on performance, or indirectly by changing the coefficient of the capital constraint. However, the direction of both the indirect and direct effects is as expected in all cases. Apparently, human and social capital factors generate and explain most of the relevant heterogeneity in the sample. I conclude that capital constraints apparently generate imperfectness of investment opportunities in terms of size and/or timing.

Conclusion

The theoretical debate about the relationship between financial capital constraints and entrepreneur performance has generated two opposing views: (i) capital markets are perfect and therefore do not hinder entrepreneurs in their required investments with regard to the levels and timeliness, *vis-à-vis* (ii) capital markets do not supply the right amount of capital to entrepreneurs due to asymmetric information. Empirical evidence has largely supported the second view: capital constraints do hinder entrepreneurial performance (see Table 8.1).

I have already pointed out several drawbacks pertaining to the empirical strategies that have produced this evidence. First, since the relationship between assets (obtained in a specific manner) and performance is considered, the possibility of obtaining external finance remains unconsidered.

Second, the possible discontinuity in the relationship is not taken into account in this approach. I illustrated these first two drawbacks by a simple model set-up. Third, 'family assets' is generally not an exogenous variable. Finally, assets are generally badly reported in individual survey research and are therefore unreliable. Alternatives such as the inheritance or windfall gains approaches have not greatly alleviated these concerns.

The chapter discussed a recent application of a different method to evaluate the effect of (perceivably) experiencing capital constraints on entrepreneurial performance that does not suffer from all the problems that were encountered in previous studies with the same objective. Nevertheless, this study confirms that initial capital constraints and the implied suboptimal investment possibilities significantly hinder entrepreneurs in their performance.

A couple of issues, however, remain to be resolved. First, the extent of capital constraints experienced by entrepreneurs is an endogenous variable in the entrepreneurial performance equation, no matter how many qualified control variables are entered into the performance equation. Accounting for this by means of instrumental variables or any of the other suitable approaches has as yet been underexplored.

Second, these results are indicative of the effect on performance of whether an entrepreneur has experienced capital constraints. Future research based on a survey that quantifies the *extent* of capital constraints on a continuous scale, where β could range anywhere between zero and one, might give further insight into the effects of capital constraints. Data on the individual demand and supply of external capital might be informative to this end.

An additional concern I have about previous estimates of the effect of capital constraints on business performance, including those obtained in our own study, is that the effect (or correlation) measured does not account for or measure the (extent of) substitutability between capital constraints and other factors of influence such as education. The latter has prevented the measurement of the distinct effect of each separate factor, if education simultaneously impacts capital constraints (negatively) and performance (positively).

A recent study that addresses most of these issues is Parker and van Praag (2004). They estimate the effect of capital constraints on the incomes of Dutch entrepreneurs by using an instrumental variables approach while they account for the endogenous nature of schooling. Their finding is supportive of the finding from the recent application discussed in this Chapter: capital constraints bind.

Notes

1. For instance, Evans and Jovanovic (1989); Holtz-Eakin et al. (1994b); Lindh and Ohlsson (1996); Blanchflower and Oswald (1998); Dunn and Holtz-Eakin (2000); Henley (2004). See also Chapter 3.

2. See, for example, Evans and Jovanovic (1989); Bates (1990); Cooper et al. (1994); Holtz-Eakin et al. (1994a); Cressy (1996); Lindh and Ohlsson (1996); Burke et al. (2002); Cowling et al. (2004); Hurst and Lusardi (2004); and Chapter 6 of this book.
3. However, Holtz-Eakin et al. (1994a) seem to have dealt with this issue in a neat way: by controlling for (i) whether the inheritance donor is an entrepreneur too and (ii) a measure of firm performance prior to the receipt of the inheritance.
4. Though both participation in a lottery and selection for entrepreneurship are related to risk attitude and therefore to each other (see Chapter 4).
5. It is assumed that the positive effects of θ_i on A_i and k_i^* just cancel out: capital need $(k_i^* - A_i)$ is independent of θ_i and does not affect β_i or P.
6. We considered the 7% + 17% of the sample who answered yes as an alternative indicator of capital constraints. This weakened the result considerably. The same holds for the alternative specification where the first answer is translated into $\beta_i = 1$, the second into $\beta_i = 0.5$ and where the third is still equivalent to $\beta_i = 0$.
7. Empirical support for the selection of relevant components of human capital is found in, for instance, Bates (1990); Cooper et al. (1994); Cressy (1996); Pennings et al. (1998); and Chapter 6. Education enters the analyses as a dummy variable, differentiating the highly educated business founders (academic/higher vocational formal education) from the lower-educated ones.
8. Empirical evidence on relevant manifestations of social capital can be found in Brüderl and Preisendorfer (1998); Pennings et al. (1998); and Bosma et al. (2004).
9. The factors resulting from factor analysis are standard normally distributed.
10. Using information channels is closely related to social capital, though it is usually not considered as such. It reflects the strategy used to retrieve relevant information from relationships. Since the relationships themselves do not occur naturally and since the information retrieval within each relationship somehow indicates the intensity of the relationship, the resulting factors are labelled as elements of social capital.
11. A third hypothesis that would cause a downward bias is the overinvestment *overconfidence* hypothesis. Overconfident entrepreneurs might aim at larger than efficient amounts of start-up capital. Without access to the desired amount, they feel constrained and report so. Unfortunately, we are unable to test this hypothesis which would again lead to an underestimate of the effect of the capital constraint on performance.
12. The firm size and industry distributions of the 1994 and 1997 are representative of the population of firms considered.
13. The profit measure has zero as lower bound: negative profits are not observed. Therefore, the equation is estimated using Tobit regressions. For duration, we apply a log-logistic survival model.

PART V

CONCLUSIONS

9 Summary, conclusions and policy recommendations

This chapter's first section gives a summarized overview of the preceding chapters of the book. In the next section I provide the main conclusions from combining the findings of these preceding chapters. Policy recommendations that arise from the results are discussed in the concluding section.

Summary

Chapter 1 is the first chapter of the introductory part (Part I) of the book. It addresses why and how this book uncovers the magic of successful entrepreneurship in an economic context. Individual determinants of successful entrepreneurship are investigated, because insight into these determinants may lead to better policy measures to increase the quality and number of entrepreneurs. These types of policy measures are important since they increase the economic benefits of successful entrepreneurship, that is, increase labour demand and economic development, and decrease the social, private and psychological costs of unsuccessful entrepreneurship. The established scientific knowledge base of entrepreneurship lacks full insight into these determinants.

This insight is gained in the following manner. Chapter 2, the second and last chapter of Part I, reviews some historical contributions to the theory of successful entrepreneurship in such a way that it provides a more thorough understanding of the entrepreneur, entrepreneurial success and the issues that are important in empirical research in this field. The relevant ideas of Cantillon, Say, Marshall, Schumpeter, Knight and Kirzner are reviewed. As of the eighteenth century, an important economic function was imputed to the entrepreneur, both in society and in the firm. The entrepreneur contributes to society and the firm by completing his specific tasks. The perceived tasks and contributions differ more or less among the six authors named. This is due, on the one hand, to differences in their perception of the economic system and/or the firm and, on the other, to differences in their definition of the entrepreneur's function. As a result, they identify different determinants of entrepreneurial ability or personality needed for successful performance. Moreover, the returns to successful entrepreneurship vary and the motive to start up as an entrepreneur differs too. The empirical analyses in the subsequent chapters reflect these views.

The review of these historical contributions indicates strongly that opportunity and willingness are distinct requirements for an individual to decide to become an entrepreneur (see Chapter 3). Moreover, the empirical definitions of entrepreneurial success used in Parts III and IV, that is, survival, labour demand, profit and income, stem from the same source.

Several of the historical contributions emphasize the role of capital constraints for the start-up and performance of business ventures. The role of capital constraints is analysed empirically for the start-up probability (Chapter 3) as well as for entrepreneurial performance (Chapter 8).

All historical contributors to the economic thought of entrepreneurship also discuss the role of risk attitude explicitly. An empirical analysis of the role of risk attitude for entrepreneurship is discussed in Chapters 4 and 5. The classic economists reviewed in Chapter 2 also assign an important influence on entrepreneurship to human capital in general and education in particular. The effect of human capital factors, that is, education as well as labour experience, are analysed in the empirical chapters. Chapter 7 is notable in this respect. Hence, Chapter 2 provides an important source of inspiration for the empirical analyses reported in the remainder of the book. Diverging views in several respects between the various scholars are tested in the empirical chapters.

The rest of the book is largely empirical. Part II (Chapters 3 and 4) investigates the factors affecting entrepreneurial start-ups, whereas Part III (Chapters 5 and 6) and Part IV (Chapters 7 and 8) analyse the factors that affect entrepreneurial success. Table 9.1 summarizes the results from each empirical chapter.

Chapter 3 empirically investigates the determinants of the decision to start as an entrepreneur. The contributions of the factors 'willingness' and 'opportunity' to this decision are disentangled; see the first and second columns of Table 9.1. The estimates of the bivariate probit model indicate that the number of individuals willing to become self-employed is far higher than the number of individuals who have the opportunity to do so. The number of entrepreneurial start-ups among young white males in the United States would increase almost sevenfold if everyone who wished to start had the opportunity to do so. Opportunity is determined by own capital and by entrepreneurial ability. Own capital significantly affects the opportunity to become self-employed: we have found clear evidence for the presence of a capital constraint. Moreover, by allowing opportunity to depend also on entrepreneurial ability, we investigated how capital-constrained individuals obtain their opportunity to start.

We found that the opportunity to start was affected by certain human capital variables. Opportunity is an increasing function of age; the older a young man in the sample is, the more opportunity he has. Moreover, each year of former experience in entrepreneurship increases the probability of having sufficient opportunity to start by more than 5 per cent for the average young white American male. Other human capital variables, which are important determinants of an individual's probability of wage employment, such as education and general labour experience, do not affect opportunity. We find willingness to be affected by some psychological character traits of individuals as well as by someone's employment history.

As capital seems to be a necessary requirement for becoming self-employed (for starters without experience) and since willingness is not a constraining factor, we conclude that the US evidence supports Knight's ideas. A first start in entrepreneurship requires ownership of assets or collateral. The additional finding that certain aspects of entrepreneurial ability are capable of serving as a substitute for owned capital is in accordance with the related ideas of Say. Schumpeter's vision is not supported empirically; motivational factors are not the prime constraints in the supply of entrepreneurship.

Chapter 4 focuses on the effect of risk aversion on the decision to become an entrepreneur. Using three measures of risk aversion that are explicitly related to microeconomic utility theory, I find that entrepreneurship is indeed discouraged by the individual degree of risk aversion; see Table 9.1 for this and other findings from the Chapter 4 analysis based on a sample of Dutch labour force participants. The evidence is consistent with the historical theoretical contributions by Cantillon, Say, Marshall and Knight discussed in Chapter 2. However, the result obtained is based on some rather strong assumptions: the three risk-aversion measures are measured (long) after the decision to become an entrepreneur has been taken, and it is tacitly assumed that they describe an individual trait that is constant over life. But if risk aversion by whatsoever definition is reduced by the experience of entrepreneurship or by income or wealth, this would certainly alter the interpretation of the results.

Part III is devoted to the explanation and understanding of entrepreneurship success or venture performance. Chapter 5 develops a theoretical and empirical model that explains business formation and size in the Netherlands. Labour demand or the ensuing firm size is used as an indicator of success. In other words, the decision to start and entrepreneurial success are explained simultaneously. Hence, this chapter provides a link between Parts II and III.

The theoretical part of the chapter deals with the following situation. An individual who is part of the active labour force chooses to start up as an entrepreneur earning an uncertain amount of profit whenever his expected utility level as an entrepreneur compares favourably to the expected utility

Table 9.1 Key research results

	Chapter									
	3		4	5		6		7	8	
Country	US		NL	NL		US		US	NL	
Start/success	Start		Start	Start	Success	Success		Success	Success	
Dependent variable	Opportunity	Willingness	Start	Start	Labour demand	Duration	Duration*	Income	Profit	Duration
						Forced	Choice			
Variable										
Risk aversion	n/a	n/a	---	---	n/a	n/a	n/a	n/a	n/a	n/a
Capital (constraint)	+++	n/a	+++	n/a	n/a	0	0	n/a	(--)	(--)
Father self-employed	n/a	n/a	+++	++	0	n/a	n/a	n/a	n/a	n/a
Father education/job level	n/a	n/a	+++	+++	0	n/a	n/a	n/a	n/a	n/a
Age	--	++	n/a	n/a	--	+++	++	n/a	0	0
Age squared	++	--	n/a	n/a	n/a	-	0	n/a	0	0
Female	n/a	n/a	---	---	0	n/a	n/a	---	n/a	n/a
Intelligence	n/a	n/a	++	+++	0	n/a	n/a	+++	n/a	n/a
Education level/years	0	0	n/a	++	+++	n/a	n/a	+++	++	0

Vocational schooling	n/a	+++	+++	0	n/a	n/a	n/a	n/a
Labour experience	n/a	0	0	0	--	n/a	+	0
Self-employment experience	++	0	0	0	0	n/a	++	0
Industry experience	n/a	n/a	n/a	+++	++	n/a	++	++
Unemployed	0	0	0	--	0	n/a	n/a	n/a

Note: Duration* refers to the survival duration of entrepreneurs where two competing hazards are distinguished. The left-hand side column summarizes the results for the case that the only possible hazard would be a forced exit from entrepreneurship, whereas the right-hand side column summarizes the results for the case that the only possible hazard would be a voluntary exit from entrepreneurship.

level as an employee. Otherwise, he becomes an employee in one of the entrepreneurs' firms, earning the common fixed wage rate. The outcome of this comparison, that is, the relative utility derived from entrepreneurship, depends on an individual's entrepreneurial ability and risk attitude. Individual success as an entrepreneur, as measured by firm size, is dependent on ability. Entrepreneurial ability depends on a vector of individual characteristics. The endogenous wage rate establishes equilibrium on the labour market.

The theoretical model is structurally estimated on a sample of Dutch labour force participants. Entrepreneurial ability is determined by measurable individual characteristics such as social background and education. Risk attitude is supposed to be a function of the individual reservation price for participation in a particular fictitious lottery.

The estimation results of the structural model are as follows. Consistent with Chapter 4, risk aversion has a significant negative effect on the choice for entrepreneurship. Men appear to have more entrepreneurial ability than women. The estimates of the structural model reveal furthermore that parental background, and in particular the occupational status of the father, affects successful entrepreneurship. If one's father is a manager, the positive effect is largest. Individuals with fathers who were self-employed have better opportunities on the entrepreneurial market, perhaps due to the availability of a family business that can be acquired. If the father had a job at the lowest level, for which no particular skills are needed, entrepreneurial success is more difficult to achieve. Both intelligence and schooling (level and type) are important determinants of successful entrepreneurship. It appears that the determinants of successful entrepreneurship, with the current definition of success, are quite similar to the general findings with respect to the factors affecting individual wage levels, that is, performance as an employee.

The major limitation is that the empirical analysis is based on several unrealistic assumptions: a single wage rate; homogeneous employee productivity; full-time employment only; and a closed economy in which all firms owe their existence to the talents of the entrepreneur. This is a serious limitation, although the same empirical results are obtained by means of a reduced-form empirical analysis. Second, the causality of the correlation between risk attitude and entrepreneurship is not proven, since risk attitude is measured after occupations have been chosen. I assume risk attitude to be constant over time, but I am not in a position to prove that assumption (see Chapter 4).

In order to be able to include the results from Chapter 5 into Table 9.1, and also to gain some more insight into the results just described, I also estimate entry into entrepreneurship and entrepreneurial firm size separately in reduced form.[1] The main additional findings are the following. The effect of gender on successful entrepreneurship appears to be due to its effect on entry; there is no significant difference in success between men and women. But the probability that a woman becomes an entrepreneur is significantly lower. The findings of the structural model with respect to parental background appear to be caused by the same effect; the father's occupational position mentioned affects entrepreneurship entry, not firm size. The same is true for the effect of intelligence. Educational level has a positive effect on both entry and success. A comparison of the empirical results with the historical theories easily leads to the conclusion that the model outcome is closest to the ideas of Marshall.

Chapter 6 is the second chapter of Part III devoted to finding general determinants of entrepreneurship success. The objective of Chapter 6 is to find significant determinants of survival and success (defined in a specific manner) in entrepreneurship. To this end the life stories of the Chapter 3 subsample of US entrepreneurs are continued; the determinants of their entrepreneurial persistence are empirically derived. A distinction is made between voluntary and compulsory exits from entrepreneurship. Only a compulsory exit is seen as a lack of success. In this way, determinants of success are derived.

There is little theory or empirical evidence about person-oriented determinants of business survival. I therefore derive potential survival determinants from empirical evidence concerning related issues by means of a statistical relationship developed for the purpose. This also results in hypotheses about the qualitative effect of regressor variables on self-employment duration. A priori determinants of success versus failure in business are adopted from the historical theories of Chapter 2.

The main results are as follows (see Table 9.1). The hazard for exit from entrepreneurship is an increasing function of time in business up until 27 months and then decreases. There are some important human capital determinants of business survival and success. Business duration is positively affected by age at the start. Older starters are more successful as well as more motivated to continue. General labour experience is insignificant as a determinant of survival in business but has a significant positive effect on the hazard of a voluntary transition from self-employment; the probability of leaving self-employment is higher for more experienced individuals, probably due to the availability of better alternative career options. Specific experience in the industry or in the occupation in which one is self-employed also increases business duration. Simulations show that industry experience decreases the probability of business failure. Other human capital determinants, such as education and entrepreneurship experience have no influence on success in business, that is, on preventing forced exits from business. Whether a starting entrepreneur possesses capital, either assets or real estate, is of no importance for explaining business survival or success. However, one's labour market position at the start is influential: unemployed starters are significantly less successful.

These results are broadly in line with the hypotheses about the qualitative effects of regressor variables on duration that were derived from empirical evidence. Comparison of the historical success indicators to the results shows that the current US situation supports the ideas of Say, Marshall, Schumpeter and Knight, with a few exceptions. Marshall's ideas deviate the most. Education, capital and family background are all insignificant in this analysis.

Part IV discusses two specific determinants of entrepreneurial success in more depth: human and financial capital. Thus, I focus on the two most influential and policy-relevant factors affecting venture performance. In particular, I try to measure the effects of schooling and capital constraints at the time the business venture was started. Chapter 7 investigates the effect of human capital (US sample), Chapter 8 analyses the effect of capital constraints (Dutch sample).

Regarding education, and based on a literature review, Chapter 7 explores the idea that the returns to education for entrepreneurs need to be measured with the same methodological rigour as studies for employees. Especially, the neglect of the endogenous nature of schooling is a problem and would possibly lead to underestimating the effect of education on performance. Compared with the vast literature on rates of return to schooling for wage and salary workers, the literature on entrepreneurs' rates of return is much less developed. I discuss a recent study in which I estimate the effect of schooling on education while accounting for this endogeneity problem (see Table 9.1). This study (together with the already mentioned study by Parker and van Praag, 2004) is the first in the field of entrepreneurship that applies IV techniques and thereby accounts for the potential endogeneity of education. The results from both studies imply that previous estimates have indeed been biased downwards. Do these results then shed an entirely new light on the conclusions from the literature with respect to the effect of education on venture performance? To answer this question I compare the findings from Chapter 7 with respect to the RTE with the conclusions from a meta-analysis of previous studies into the effect of education on entrepreneurship (selection and) performance that we were able to gather.

The first conclusion from the meta-analysis was that education has a significantly positive impact on entrepreneurs' performance. This conclusion is supported and thus maintained. The second conclusion was that the estimated rate of return to education for entrepreneurs was 6.1 per cent on average. This conclusion is not supported: the RTE for entrepreneurs are much higher: the estimate in Chapter 7, pertaining to the United States, yields an RTE of 14.2 per cent. The study by Parker and van Praag confirms this result for the Netherlands.

The third conclusion of the previous literature base was that the RTE are slightly higher for entrepreneurs than for employees in the United States, whereas the opposite was found for Europe. Neither in the United States, nor in Europe was this difference in the RTE between entrepreneurs and employees found to be significant. This conclusion is not supported by the results from Chapter 7: the returns for entrepreneurs in the United States are shown to be much higher than those for employees (respectively, 14.2 and 10.7 per cent). This turnaround finding must be somewhat puzzling in the light of the traditional studies that test screening hypotheses: apparently entrepreneurs cannot be maintained as an assumedly unscreened control group.

Of course, the use of instrumental variables is not without critique; nor is the choice of the instruments that were applied in Chapter 7. The use of family background characteristics as instruments for education has been criticized by Card (1999), who states that it could be possible that family background variables have an additional and separate effect on income. Although we have not found evidence of this spurious effect, I argue that, in order to validate the results found, more analyses in this spirit should be performed with different sets of instruments. Besides the use of different instruments, the use of other identification strategies such as twin studies and field experiments are of utmost relevance.

One other, but related, issue of concern is the low 'explanatory power' of the determinants of the entrepreneurs' income equation. In Chapter 7 we can explain only 28 per cent of the variance in entrepreneurial income by the observed factors compared to almost 50 per cent in the employee part of the labour force. It is therefore possible that we are missing some important determinants of entrepreneurial performance. The full exploitation of human, social and financial capital as determinants of entrepreneur performance should therefore be started. Education, for instance, has been defined almost exclusively as the level of education. Future research should also focus on the specific direction and context of the education followed (vocational studies, technical studies, subjects studied, or specific entrepreneurship-oriented courses, and so on). Chapter 5 yields some indication that this would be a fruitful route.

As for the effect of financial capital constraints on venture performance, investigated in Chapter 8, the conclusion is that capital constraints lead to a suboptimal use of investment opportunities and thereby to a weaker venture performance (see Table 9.1). This result emerges no matter what (suboptimal) estimation strategy is employed. Nevertheless, the state of the art of studies into the effect of financial capital constraints on venture performance is also somewhat disappointing. I argued in Chapter 8 that most previous studies have not actually measured the effect of capital constraints, but rather the effect of assets or of an (random) increase in assets. The application discussed in Chapter 8 is the first that measures the effect of capital *constraints* on venture performance. They turned out to be binding. However, neither this particular application nor any of the others has measured capital constraints on a continuous scale, or has addressed the potential endogenous nature or the biasing effect of unobserved heterogeneity of capital constraints for the explanation of venture performance in a satisfactory manner. This is important because there can be many spurious relationships between capital constraints and venture performance. For instance, banks screen (prospective) entrepreneurs based, among others, on factors that remain unobserved for the researcher. These factors are likely to affect not only business loans and thereby capital constraints but also venture performance. Otherwise, the banker would not use such characteristics as a selection criterion. However, the negative effect of a very ugly scar (for instance) on business loans and business performance would not entail a causal effect of capital constraints on venture performance. This causal effect, that is, the effect of a suboptimal investment strategy due to financial constraints, is what is of interest here.

Parker and van Praag (2004) explore these ideas further and they still find that capital constraints do hinder the entrepreneur's performance.

To summarize Part IV, I discussed some first contributions to the measurement of the effects of education and capital constraints on the performance of entrepreneurs. By using more recently developed estimation strategies, we find results that lead to different conclusions from previous research for the effect of education, but not so much for the effect of capital constraints. However, these outcomes should be interpreted with great caution, since $n = 2$ which is somewhat meagre, to say the least.

Conclusions

In this section I shall review the results that are summarized in Table 9.1 in a different manner. Whereas the summary discussed these results per chapter, that is, per column, I shall now discuss them per determinant, that is, per (group of) row(s). For each subject, I shall discuss the current knowledge, the state of the art of research into the subject, the limitations of my own research as well as ideas for future research.

Risk aversion

The debate about the role of an individual's risk attitude for the decision to become an entrepreneur and for entrepreneurial success has quite a long history in economics (see Chapter 2). Not only have Cantillon, Say, Marshall, Schumpeter and Knight already put forth a theory about risk and entrepreneurship: later, well-known formalized theoretical contributions to the economic theory of entrepreneurship, such as Kanbur (1979) and Kihlstrom and Laffont (1979) have also included such theories in formalized models. Van Praag and Cramer (2001) attempted to extend such modelling a little bit further in a more realistic direction (see Chapter 5).

Empirical testing of the effect of risk attitude on entrepreneurship has been difficult, not to say impossible, for a long time because of the difficulties involved when trying to measure an individual's risk attitude. Van Praag and Cramer (2001) and Cramer et al. (2002) have been the first to measure (the effect of) risk attitude empirically (see Chapters 4 and 5). We define risk aversion in a manner that is consistent with utility theory (see Chapter 4). We have measured the effect of risk attitude only on the decision to start up as an entrepreneur, not on success.

We find strong evidence that risk debars people from becoming entrepreneurs. This evidence, though subject to various limitations, is consistent with most of the theoretical advances as well as with later empirical evidence using alternative (and perhaps better) measures of risk aversion (see Ekelund et al., 2000). Note that we have not yet investigated the effect of risk attitude on entrepreneurial performance.

The main limitation of the empirical measurement of risk aversion that we employ is timing: we measure individuals' risk attitudes long after they have taken the decision to become employees. This is problematic if an individual's risk attitude is subject to changes over time, for instance, caused by experience, aging, or having been an entrepreneur for a long time. More research into how and due to what causes individual risk attitudes vary over time would be desirable (see also Hartog et al., 2002).

Another limitation to our studies reported in Chapters 4 and 5 is the definition of risk attitude in general. It is likely that individuals would have various risk attitudes towards various sorts of risk: one could behave according to a different risk attitude when participating in a lottery from when climbing a very dangerous mountain or from when making a risky career choice. In other words, do individuals have a single or do they have multiple risk attitudes? And if people have multiple risk attitudes, how should we measure properly the risk attitude that is related to business risks that are incurred when one becomes an entrepreneur? This would serve in my opinion as a fruitful area for future research.

Capital
The theoretical debate about the relationship between financial capital constraints and entrepreneur performance has advanced two opposing

views: (i) capital markets are perfect and therefore do not hinder entrepreneurs in their required investments with regard to levels and timeliness, *vis-à-vis* (ii) capital markets do not supply the right amounts of capital to entrepreneurs due to asymmetric information. The scholars whose theories have been discussed in Chapter 2 expressed these two opposing views a long time ago: Schumpeter and Kirzner adhere to the first view, whereas Marshall and Say are obvious proponents of the second view. Empirical evidence has largely supported the second view: capital constraints do debar individuals from starting up as an entrepreneur. Chapter 3 even shows that a lack of capital is the major factor that hinders people from exploiting an opportunity to become an entrepreneur: for instance, only a huge number of years of self-employment experience can make up for a lack of capital, if at all (see Chapter 3).

Not only do capital constraints hinder people from becoming entrepreneurs, but they also handicap those individuals who have found an opportunity to start (see Table 9.1). The evidence from the US study in Chapter 6 seems to be the exception rather than the rule (see Table 8.1): most studies have shown that a lack of capital at the start-up phase hinders the performance of entrepreneurs, whatever performance measure is employed.

I have pointed out several drawbacks pertaining to the empirical strategies that have produced this evidence, including the evidence obtained by myself and various co-authors as reported in Chapters 3, 4, 6 and, to a lesser extent, also Chapter 8. First, since the relationship between assets (obtained in a specific manner) and performance is considered, the possibility of obtaining external finance remains unconsidered in most of these studies (and also in Chapters 3, 4 and 6). Second, the possible discontinuity in the relationship is not taken into account: it could well be that more capital helps entrepreneurial success to a certain extent but that the 'more is better' argument does not hold across the entire spectrum (see also Hurst and Lusardi, 2004). A third drawback of the methods generally used to obtain the result that capital constraints bind is that 'family assets' is not an exogenous variable. A fourth drawback, finally, is that assets in general are badly reported in individual survey research and are therefore unreliable (see the discussion in Chapter 4).

I discussed a recent application by van Praag et al. (2003) of a different method to evaluate the effect of (perceivably) experiencing capital constraints on entrepreneurial performance. This study does not suffer from all the problems that were encountered in previous studies with the same objective though it has some limitations of its own (see Chapter 8). Nevertheless, it confirms that initial capital constraints and the implied suboptimal investment possibilities significantly hinder entrepreneurs in their performance.

A couple of issues, however, are not yet resolved in the Chapter 8 application. First, the extent of capital constraints experienced by entrepreneurs is an endogenous variable in the entrepreneurial performance equation, no matter how many qualified control variables are entered into the performance equation. Accounting for this by means of instrumental variables or any of the other suitable approaches has as yet been underexplored. Second, the results derived in Chapter 8 are indicative of the effect on performance of whether an entrepreneur has experienced capital constraints. It does not quantify the *extent* of capital constraints on a continuous scale. This might give further insight into the (possibly non-linear) effects of capital constraints. An additional concern I have about previous estimates of the effect of capital constraints on business performance, including those by the study in Chapter 8, is that the effect (or correlation) measured does not account for or measure the (extent of) substitutability between capital constraints and other factors of influence such as education. The latter has prevented the measurement of the distinct effect of each separate factor, in case education would simultaneously impact capital constraints (negatively) and performance (positively).

The study I already mentioned by Parker and van Praag (2004) accounts for the following three concerns: (i) it measures capital constraints on a continuous scale; (ii) capital constraints are treated as endogenous and possibly subject to biases as a consequence of unobserved individual characteristics (that affect both capital constraints and performance); and (iii) capital constraints are treated as being possibly interrelated with education.

The effect of capital constraints on performance remains negative and significant in this analysis: the more capital constrained an entrepreneur is at the time of inception of the business venture, the weaker his performance will be (in terms of income). Furthermore, capital constraints indeed turn out to be endogenous or affected by the same unobserved characteristics that also affect performance.

The study by Parker and van Praag (2004) comes close to how we should measure the effect of capital constraints on performance, at least in my opinion. It would be valuable if more research were carried out, pertaining to different countries and with different sets of instruments for capital constraints or employing other suitable empirical strategies to verify the current result.

Parental background
Two parental background variables show up quite often in research into the determinants of entrepreneurship in general: (i) whether the father

(sometimes the mother) was self-employed or independent himself and (ii) the education or job level of the father (and sometimes the mother). Table 9.1 shows that these parental background characteristics influence the probability of starting up as an entrepreneur, but not entrepreneurial performance. People are more likely to become entrepreneurs if their father was also an entrepreneur and/or if their father had a higher qualified job or a higher level of education.

The positive effect of a self-employed father on the decision to become an entrepreneur has been found more often in the entrepreneurship literature, whereas the evidence about the effect of a self-employed father on entrepreneurship success has been totally mixed. Moreover, the explanations that researchers seek for the effect of an entrepreneurial father on (successful) entrepreneurship have been mixed, too. Some attribute the effect to 'entrepreneur genes', that is, nature, whereas others have attributed it to 'entrepreneurial atmosphere at home', that is, nurture. Still others attribute the positive effect to the possibility of taking over a family venture; this possibility is not available to those who do not have an entrepreneurial parent. However, these explanations are as yet suggestions only. A better understanding of the effect of a self-employed father on the propensity to become an entrepreneur as well as on performance should be gained by using an alternative research design, for instance research on twins or adopted children.

The positive effect of a more highly educated father/mother on the start-up probability is also difficult to interpret. Table 9.1 shows the effect to have been established for the Netherlands in one data set only (Chapters 4 and 5). We have seen in Chapter 7 that the effect of parental education on an entrepreneur's performance can be explained as follows: higher-educated fathers produce higher-educated children (see Table 7A.1) and these higher-educated individuals become better-performing entrepreneurs (Table 7.1). Hence, additional research is required to understand the relationship between parental background and entrepreneurship more fully.

Age
The evidence concerning starting age is quite uniform, not only across the various chapters of this book, but also more in general. It is important to note that the evidence about the optimal age at start-up is obtained while controlling for general (and sometimes specific sorts of) labour experience. Controlling for experience is relevant as there is a positive effect of experience on performance and a strong correlation between age and experience.

In general, we find that there is an inverted U-shaped relationship between starting age and performance. Its peak is in most cases around the (starting) age of 34. People starting below that age show lower average survival chances and incomes, whereas people starting at higher ages have less opportunity for growth and also lower average incomes. This finding holds across countries and sexes.

Gender

Like almost all other empirical studies that estimate the effect of gender on the probability of becoming an entrepreneur, the studies included in this book reveal that females are less inclined than males to start up as entrepreneurs. This could be caused by various factors influencing labour market preferences that usually remain unobserved and that are different for men and women, such as risk attitude, business acumen and the preference for a specific work–life balance. In other words, females could be less *willing* than males to become entrepreneurs.

A second possible explanation is that females, for whatever reason, experience more serious impediments than males when they try to become entrepreneurs: females might have more difficulties to obtaining start-up capital; they might find it more difficult to encounter profitable clients due to a smaller professional network or due to labour market discrimination. In other words, females could have fewer *opportunities* than males to become entrepreneurs.

However, it could also be the case that it is not so much the preferences or the constraints that are different for females than for males, but that there is a difference between the sexes in the likely expected utility (or income) in entrepreneurship relative to wage employment. In other words, females would have a competitive advantage over males in wage employment.

As yet, we do not understand whether it is the willingness, the opportunity, or the competitive advantage argument, or a combination, that best explains why such a small fraction of entrepreneurs is female.

Perhaps, some light is shed on this occupational choice – gender – issue, by considering the differences in performance between males and females. With few exceptions, of which one is included in this book (that is, in Chapter 5), entrepreneurial performance is observed to be weaker for females than for males. For instance, in Chapter 7 we find that income per hour is 66 per cent higher for male than for female entrepreneurs. This implies that entrepreneurial incomes for females lag behind those for males by a substantial 40 per cent.[2] Moreover, the same table shows that the wage difference between female and male wage employees is much smaller: females earn 19 per cent lower wages than males. Other studies that have investigated the gender wage gap for entrepreneurs and employees reach a similar conclusion (van der Sluis et al., 2003): the gap is larger in the entrepreneurial sector of the labour market than in the wage sector. These observations give some support to the competitive advantage argument for why we observe so few female entrepreneurs.

It would be interesting to find out why females have a competitive disadvantage in the entrepreneurial sector of the labour market. Could it be caused by the fact that successful entrepreneurship can only be achieved by having very long working weeks and that females work fewer hours on average? Again, future research should shed light on these questions.

Education
When we measure the effect of education on the income (performance) of entrepreneurs with the same empirical rigour as is employed for the measurement of this effect for wage workers, we find interesting results (see Chapter 7): (i) the RTE for entrepreneurs are much higher than previously thought: about 15 per cent. Moreover (ii) the RTE for entrepreneurs seem to be substantially higher than those for employees.

We propose a simple explanation for this result: entrepreneurs have more freedom to optimize their use of education. Entrepreneurs are not constrained by rules from superiors and can decide how to put their education to its most productive use. In contrast, the organizational structure surrounding an employee makes it difficult to optimize the productive effect of education. Besides, the organization cannot adapt its structure to every individual due to organizational inertia and individual incompatibilities. This difference in ability to optimize the productivity of education for entrepreneurs and employees might therefore be an explanation for the higher RTE for entrepreneurs. The finding is contrary to some casual 'conventional wisdom' that entrepreneurs do not need schooling to be successful. More research, also employing different empirical strategies, should be carried out to confirm (or falsify) the result we found and to better understand what explains this result.

Furthermore, we find mixed evidence concerning the effect of education on the probability of becoming an entrepreneur. The majority of relevant studies included in this volume, however, indicate the effect to be insignificant: education does not determine someone's choice for entrepreneurship (versus wage employment). This is consistent with the results from the meta-analysis discussed in Chapter 7: 75 per cent of the studies explaining the probability of becoming an entrepreneur by means of education (among other factors) find an insignificant effect.

Finally, research into the effect of specific sorts of education on entrepreneurship outcomes is still in its infancy (see van der Sluis et al., 2003) although Lazear (2004), Wagner (2002) and Silva (2004) have recently performed interesting studies in this area. The results from Chapters 4 and 5 indicate that vocational schooling promotes the decision to become an entrepreneur but that it does not enhance performance. However, the causality of this effect on selection is questionable. The same chapters show that a science-oriented education has a positive correlation with success in entrepreneurship.

General and specific labour experience
The returns on general labour market experience are mixed in most models explaining entrepreneurial performance. The returns on previous entrepreneurship experience are ambiguous too. However, little research has addressed the issue of endogeneity in this respect, which is obviously present: the group of individuals who start again as entrepreneurs are most probably not a random selection of the population of entrepreneurs. For instance, if only the best-performing entrepreneurs opt to restart, the effect of self-employment experience would be an overestimate of the real effect. Therefore, the restart decision should be analysed more carefully. Chapter 3 indicated that self-employment experience increases the opportunity of becoming an entrepreneur (again) significantly. It should, however, be noted that this result pertains to the United States. In Europe, the effect is not as positive due to the much stronger stigma effect of previous entrepreneurship (failure).

The only unambiguous result with respect to experience is the positive effect of labour experience within the industry: the more within-industry experience an individual has gathered before becoming an entrepreneur in that specific industry, the better his chances of success are. We do not know yet to what extent this effect is explained by the underlying professional network, by the fact that such entrepreneurs start, while having clients already, because there are others who ask them to do so (previous employers or clients of these employers), or whether the industry experience generates higher productivity.

Unemployment
One's personal (un)employment situation at the start of a venture affects success significantly. Entrepreneurship entry, on the other hand, reacts quite strongly to the macro measure of unemployment and not at all to the personal measure. Hence, the important relationship between self-employment and unemployment depends on whether a macro or personal indicator of the latter is selected and whether one investigates entry or success. This finding could explain the diverging results in the relevant literature.

Policy recommendations
The objective of this section is to show how these results, and also future research results of the same type, can be utilized as a scientific basis for policy evaluation and improvement. This is of interest for institutions with a mission to increase the number and quality of entrepreneurs.

The results are of interest for banks and other capital suppliers in their decision to grant loans to starters. They increase their profitability and bear less risk when they succeed either in selecting the (potentially) most successful entrepreneurs or in preparing entrepreneurs in such a way that they enhance their potential success. They are also relevant for authorities striving at more employment and economic growth through a larger number of more-qualified entrepreneurs.

The start-up determinants in the first four columns of Table 9.1 form a basis for policy measures meant to increase the number of entrepreneurs. Policy measures meant to increase the quality of entrepreneurs can be based on the success determinants in the remaining columns of the table. The implications of the results will be discussed in what follows. I shall first address the limitations of the research results as well as the (implicit) assumptions that I use such that the policy implications indeed follow from the research results.

Some limitations
The results are suitable to indicate some policy measures to improve the number and quality of entrepreneurs. However, there are some limitations:

- I do not know the 'alternative social value' of individuals who are potentially (un)successful as entrepreneurs. The results indicate who the prospective (un)successful entrepreneurs are, and according to these results I recommend whom to select or encourage and whom to discourage from becoming an entrepreneur. However, I am not in a position to judge for a particular individual whether the social benefits (costs) of his/her (un)successful entrepreneurship are higher or lower than the benefits (costs) pertaining to the alternative situation; that is, when this particular potentially (un)successful entrepreneur will not become an entrepreneur. I do not have the instruments or skills required for including this type of cost–benefit consideration in the analysis on which the policy recommendations that follow are based.
- Individual utility, happiness or job satisfaction are not taken into account in the analysis on which the policy recommendations are based. I consider what type of individuals should start in order to maximize social benefits of entrepreneurship, but I more or less disregard personal non-financial benefits of entrepreneurship versus the alternative.
- I am not aware of the meaning of failures in an uncertain world. Perhaps there is a 'social value' pertaining to unsuccessful entrepreneurship; a 'sorting period' could render valuable information. In the recommendations that follow, I take for granted that unsuccessful entrepreneurship should be prevented if possible.

Assumptions

Before I discuss the policy implications following from the results it is important to elaborate on the assumptions required to be able to have those implications follow from these results.

First, I assume that the social return of entrepreneurial activity is larger than the private return that accrues to the entrepreneur himself. Hence, on top of the utility the entrepreneur derives from his professional activities, there are some positive spin-offs from his activities, such as more employment, innovation, economic growth, or tax income. Second, I assume that the difference between the social and private benefits of entrepreneurial activity is larger than this difference is for employees. A successful entrepreneur is, for example, more likely to influence the competition in a market than is an employee. Moreover, entrepreneurs can bring new and innovative ideas more easily into the market than can employees. Third, I assume that individuals invest in schooling at a stage in their lives at which they do not yet know, in general, whether they will become entrepreneurs, or employees, or a (sequential) combination of both. As a consequence, investment in schooling is not motivated by the specific expected return when belonging to the group of entrepreneurs, but by some (weighted) average return of both employment modes. My fourth assumption is that individuals, as well as policy makers, bankers and other parties involved, have no more insight into the returns to education and the effect of capital constraints than we as researchers have.

Implications

In this last subsection of the book, I shall discuss the policy implications resulting from the findings, subject to the limitations and based on the assumptions mentioned before. The policy recommendations are organized according to the same subject categories as the conclusions.

Risk attitude Risk aversion debars people from starting a business. Assuming that risk attitude has no effect on entrepreneurship success, and knowing that a more positive attitude towards risk has a positive effect on the decision to become an entrepreneur, I recommend:

- If risk attitude can be influenced (at schools, for instance) this could increase the number of people who start up as an entrepreneur. In order to increase this number specifically in the category of successful entrepreneurs, these risk-enhancing measures should be directed to selected groups of people only (for instance, people with higher levels of education, and/or those with a science-oriented education).
- If risk attitude cannot be influenced, it would be helpful to start

enhancing entrepreneurial skills at an early stage among those people who are less risk averse. It should be possible to test individual risk attitude, for instance, when individuals enter secondary school and to encourage those with low levels of risk aversion to undergo specific training.

Age and labour market experience Entrepreneurs should not start their business venture at too young an age (say, less than 30), because starters who are too young have a lower probability of surviving: older people face a lower risk of exiting entrepreneurship both in terms of voluntary as well as in terms of compulsory exits (Chapter 3). But they should not be too old either, because the capacity to grow is less when entrepreneurship starts at an older age (Chapter 5). In particular, since it is fruitful to wait until the mid-thirties, before starting a business, and since it is worthwhile to gain some within-industry experience first, this should be recommended to individuals who wish to start at a (too) young age. Business success is more easily achieved if the entrepreneur has experience within the same industry and/or occupation as the current venture. Additional years of schooling instead of starting a business immediately would also serve to enhance the performance of these (too) young entrepreneurs.

Moreover, the social costs pertaining to entrepreneurship failures seem to be lower for entrepreneurs who have some experience in wage employment (Chapter 6): they tend to find a job quite easily after closing down their business. Therefore, social benefits are higher for start-ups among people who have some experience in wage employment as they will more easily find an alternative and not be a burden on society. Given two persons with equal (but not outstanding) entrepreneurial talents, it is preferable to offer the opportunity to start to the one with more experience in wage employment.

The fact that self-employment experience may serve as a substitute for capital and/or collateral (see Chapter 3) suggests that US banks and participation companies believe that entrepreneurship can be learned through experience (or that they can screen for superior entrepreneurship qualities by means of this indicator if they believe that its positive effect is due to unobserved heterogeneity). However, the tabulated results show mixed effects about whether experienced entrepreneurs are more successful than unexperienced ones. The common belief should be re-evaluated.

Parental background Individuals with a certain parental background, that is, with parents who are entrepreneurs and/or highly educated, are more inclined to become entrepreneurs, but they are not more successful as such than entrepreneurs with other parental backgrounds. Hence, it would be wise to pay special attention to this group aiming at better performance. For instance, it would be valuable if individuals who wish to take over the family firm were encouraged to work for an employer first (in the same industry).

Education The knowledge that the RTE are high and that education is therefore a key input in a starting enterprise, is informative for the design of educational policies and policies with respect to (selecting) starters designed by bankers and other capital suppliers. Moreover, the adequate design of tax and subsidy measures towards starters and their capital suppliers (mostly by the Ministry of Business and Economic Affairs) might also benefit from these insights.

Policy makers should be aware that the RTE for entrepreneurs are likely to be higher than those of employees.[3] Governments could take two actions regarding this new knowledge. They could invest in higher schooling for (prospective) entrepreneurs or they could invest in stimulating higher-educated individuals to opt for entrepreneurship. The first action will ensure that entrepreneurs will perform better on average, and that they will thereby generate more benefits that will accrue not only to the entrepreneur himself but also to society as a whole. This will decrease the social costs pertaining to bankruptcy accordingly. The second action appeals to the fact that, at least in Europe, entrepreneurship does not seem to be a favoured option, or even to be part of the choice set, among young people with higher education. They usually favour working in a large multinational company and do not even consider self-employment. I strongly believe in the benefits of governmental programmes to stimulate the awareness of the option of entrepreneurship to college and university students.

Further research into the character of the most beneficial types of education will lead in practice to useful insights into the design of schooling tracks that are recommended to entrepreneurs. These types of education can then further be used to recruit entrepreneurs, for instance by the Ministry of Business and Economic Affairs, and to further stimulate and facilitate these entrepreneurs, financially or otherwise, for instance by means of subsidies and (loan) guarantees.

Capital constraints The more capital an individual has at his disposal, the more opportunity he has to become an entrepreneur and to be successful. Governments should therefore take measures to improve borrowing facilities for starters as banks and participation companies seem to ration this risky market. The government has a valid incentive to create, for instance, a 'risk fund', given the positive external effects of entrepreneurship.

Unemployment It appears that low unemployment rates spontaneously improve entrepreneurship opportunities. Authorities want to reduce unemployment by stimulating entrepreneurship. The demand for entre-preneurship encouragement programmes is therefore highest when the unemployment rate is high.

An individual's labour market position just before the start of a firm is influential for success. Preferably, there should not be a period of unemployment between a former job and the start of an entrepreneurial venture. Unemployed starters perform less well. Entrepreneurs are most successful if they start their business before quitting their job as an employee. The implication is that entrepreneurs who start because or while they were unemployed at the time should be better prepared by means of training.

There are, of course, other policy measures that can be taken to increase the number of entrepreneurs. However, these do not arise from our findings. None the less, any measure to increase the number of entrepreneurs should be directed at the group of potentially successful entrepreneurs (particu-larly when the number of potentially successful entrepreneurs has been boosted as indicated in the above paragraph).

The result of improved policy measures will be the decrease of barriers to entry for potentially successful starters and the increase of useful support to those starters. This will reduce the social costs of bankruptcy and increase the social benefits of innovative enterprises.

Notes

1. The results from this analysis are not included in Chapter 5.
2. $(1-100/166)*100$.
3. I assume implicitly that individuals and policy makers share the knowledge (and common opinion) that the RTE are similar for entrepreneurs and for employees.

Bibliography

Abowd, J.M. and H.S. Farber (1982), 'Job queues and the union status of workers', *Industrial and Labour Review*, **35**, 354–67.

Angrist, J. and A. Krueger (1991), 'Does compulsory school attendance affect schooling and earnings?', *Quarterly Journal of Economics*, **106**, 979–1014.

Ashenfelter, O., C. Harmon and H. Oosterbeek (1999), 'A review of the schooling/earnings relationship with tests for publication bias', *Labour Economics*, **6**, 453–70.

Ashenfelter, O. and A. Krueger (1994), 'Estimates of the returns to schooling from a new sample of twins', *American Economic Review*, **84**(5), 1157–73.

Audretsch, D. and M. Keilbach (2003), 'Entrepreneurship capital and economic performance', CEPR Discussion Paper 3678, Centre for Economic Policy Research, London.

Barreto, H. (1989), *The Entrepreneur in Economic Theory: Disappearance and Explanation*, London: Routledge.

Bates, T. (1990), 'Entrepreneur human capital inputs and small business longevity', *Review of Economics and Statistics*, **72**(4), 551–9.

Baumol, W.J. (1968), 'Entrepreneurship in economic theory', *American Economic Review*, **58**, 64–71.

Baumol, W.J. (1993), *Entrepreneurship, Management and the Structure of Payoffs*, Cambridge, MA: MIT Press.

Behrman, J. and M. Rosenzweig (1999), 'Ability biases in schooling returns and twins: a test and new estimates', *Economics of Education Review*, **18**(2), 159–67.

Bhide, A. (1994), 'How entrepreneurs craft strategies that work', *Harvard Business Review*, March/April, 150–61.

Black, J., D. De Meza and D. Jeffreys (1996), 'House price, the supply of collateral and the enterprise economy', *Economic Journal*, **106**(434), 60–75.

Blackburn, M. and D. Neumark (1993), 'Are OLS estimates of the return to schooling biased downwards? Another look', *Review of Economics and Statistics*, **77**, 217–30.

Blanchflower, D. and B. Meyer (1994), 'A longitudinal analysis of the young self-employed in Australia and the United States', *Small Business Economics*, **6**(1), 898–921.

Blanchflower, D. and A. Oswald (1998), 'What makes an entrepreneur?', *Journal of Labor Economics*, **16**(1), 26–60.

Boadway, R., N. Marceau, M. Marchand and M. Vigneault (1998), 'Entrepreneurship, asymmetric information, and unemployment', *International Tax and Public Finance*, **5**(3), 307–27.

Bonjour, D., L. Cherkas, J. Haskel, D. Hawkes and T. Spector (2003), 'Returns to education: evidence from UK twins', *American Economic Review*, **93**(5), 1799–812.

Bosma, N., C.M. van Praag, R. Thurik and G. de Wit (2004). 'The value of human and social capital investments for the business performance of start-ups', *Small Business Economics*, **23**(3), 227–36.

Brock, W. and D. Evans (1986), *The Economics of Small Businesses: Their Role and Regulation in the US Economy*, New York: Holmes & Meier.

Brockhaus, R. (1980), 'The effect of job dissatisfaction on the decision to start a business', *Journal of Small Business Management*, **18**(1), 37–43.

Brüderl, J. and P. Preisendörfer (1998), 'Network support and success of newly founded businesses', *Small Business Economics*, **10**, 213–25.

Brüderl, J., P. Preisendörfer and R. Ziegler (1992), 'Organizational survival', *American Sociological Review*, **57**, 227–42.

Burke, A., F. FitzRoy and M. Nolan (2002), 'Self-employment wealth and job creation: the roles of gender, non-pecuniary motivation and entrepreneurial ability', *Small Business Economics*, **19**, 255–70.

Calvo, G. and S. Wellisz (1980), 'Technology, entrepreneurs and firm size', *Quarterly Journal of Economics*, **95**, 663–78.

Cantillon, R. [1755 (1979)], *Essai sur la nature du commerce en général* (Essay on the nature of commerce), Takumi Tsuda (ed.), Tokyo, Japan: Kinokuniya Book-store Co.

Card, D. (1999), 'Causal effect of education on earnings', in O. Ashenfelter and D. Card (eds), *Handbook of Labor Economics*, Vol. 3A, Amsterdam: North-Holland, pp. 1801–63.

Chandler, G. and S. Hanks (1994), 'Founder competence, the environment and venture performance', *Entrepreneurship, Theory and Practice*, **18**(3), 77–89.

Coase, R. (1937), 'The nature of the firm', *Economica*, NS, **IV**, 386–405.

Cooper, A., F. Gimeno-Gascon and C. Woo (1994), 'Initial human and financial capital as predictors of new venture performance', *Journal of Business Venturing*, **9**, 371–95.

Cowling, M., M. Taylor and P. Mitchell (2004), 'Job creators', *The Manchester School*, **72**(5), 601–17.

Cramer, J., J. Hartog, N. Jonker and C.M. van Praag (2002), 'Low risk aversion encourages the choice for entrepreneurship: an empirical test of a truism', *Journal of Economic Behavior and Organization*, **48**, 29–36.

Cressy, R. (1996), 'Are business start-ups debt-rationed?', *Economic Journal*, **106**, 1253–70.

Curran, J. and R. Burrows (1989), *Enterprise in Britain: A National Profile of Small Business Owners and the Self Employed*, London: Small Business Research Trust.

Davidson, R. and J. MacKinnon (1993), *Estimation and Inference in Econometrics*, New York: Oxford University Press.

Davidsson, P. and B. Honig (2003), 'The role of social and human capital among nascent entrepreneurs', *Journal of Business Venturing*, **18**, 301–40.

De Meza, D. and D. Webb (2000), 'Does credit rationing imply insufficient lending?', *Journal of Public Economics*, **78**(3), 215–34.

De Wit, G. (1993), 'Models of self-employment in a competitive market', *Journal of Economic Surveys*, **7**, 367–97.

Deaton, A. (2000), *The Analysis of Household Surveys*, Baltimore, MD: Johns Hopkins University Press.

Dunn, T. and D. Holtz-Eakin (2000), 'Financial capital, human capital, and the transition to self-employment: evidence from intergenerational links', *Journal of Labor Economics*, **18**(2), 282–305.

Ekelund, J., E. Johansson, M. Järvelin and D. Lichtermann (2000), 'Self-employment and risk-aversion: evidence from psychological test data', unpublished working paper, Swedish School of Economics and Business Administration, Helsinki, Sweden.

Evans, D. and B. Jovanovic (1989), 'An estimated model of entrepreneurial choice under liquidity constraints', *Journal of Political Economy*, **97**, 808–27.

Evans, D. and L. Leighton (1989), 'Some empirical aspects of entrepreneurship', *American Economic Review*, **79**, 519–35.

Evans, D. and L. Leighton (1990), 'Small business formation by unemployed and employed workers', *Small Business Economics*, **2**, 319–30.

Fazzari, S., R. Hubbard and B. Petersen (1988), 'Financing constraints and corporate investment', *Brookings Papers on Economic Activity*, 1988(1), 141–95.

Fredland, J. and R. Little (1981), 'Self-employed workers: returns to education and training', *Economics of Education Review*, **1**(3), 315–37.

Fritsch, M., U. Brixy and O. Falck (2004), 'The effect of industry, region and time on new business survival – a multi-dimensional analysis', Freiberg Working Paper 4-2004, Technical University Bergakademie Freiberg, Germany.

Griliches, Z. (1977), 'Estimating the returns to schooling: some econometric problems', *Econometrica*, **45**(1), 1–22.

Hartog, J., A. Ferrer-i-Carbonell and N. Jonker (2002), 'Linking measured risk aversion to individual characteristics', *Kyklos*, **55**(1), 3–26.

Hausman, J. (1978), 'Specification tests in econometrics', *Econometrica*, **46**, 1251–71.

Hébert, R. and A. Link (1988), *The Entrepreneur, Mainstream Views and Radical Critiques*, New York: Praeger.

Heertje, A. (1982), 'Schumpeter's model of the decay of Capitalism', Chapter 5 in H. Frisch (ed.), *Schumpeterian Economics*, New York: Praeger.

Heertje, A. (1993), 'Capitalism, socialism and democracy after fifty years', Chapter 3 in D. Bös (ed.), *Public Policy and Economic Organization*, Vol. III of *Economics in a Changing World*; proceedings of the tenth world congress (1992) of the International Economic Association, London: Macmillan.

Henley, A. (2004), 'Self-employment status: the role of state dependence and initial circumstances', *Small Business Economics*, **22**, 67–82.

Holmes, T. and A. Schmitz (1995), 'On the turnover of business firms and business managers', *Journal of Political Economy*, **103**, 1005–38.

Holtz-Eakin, D., D. Joulfaian and H. Rosen (1994a), 'Sticking it out: entrepreneurial survival and liquidity constraints', *Journal of Political Economy*, **102**, 53–75.

Holtz-Eakin, D., D. Joulfaian and H. Rosen (1994b), 'Entrepreneurial decisions and liquidity constraints', *Rand Journal of Economics*, **25**(2), 334–47.

Hornaday, J. and J. Aboud (1971), 'Characteristics of successful entrepreneurs', *Personnel Psychology*, **24**(2), 141–53.

Hurst, E. and A. Lusardi (2004), 'Liquidity constraints, household wealth and entrepreneurship', *Journal of Political Economy*, **112**(2), 319–47.

Jovanovic, B. (1982), 'Selection and the evolution of industry', *Econometrica*, **50**, 649–70.

Jovanovic, B. (1994), 'Firm formation with heterogeneous management and labour skills', *Small Business Economics*, **6**, 185–91.

Kaldor, N. (1934), 'The equilibrium of the firm', *Economic Journal*, **44**, 60–76.

Kanbur, S. (1979), 'On risk taking and the personal distribution of income', *Journal of Political Economy*, **87**, 760–97.

Kihlstrom, R. and J. Laffont (1979), 'A general equilibrium entrepreneurial theory of new firm formation based on risk aversion', *Journal of Political Economy*, **87**, 719–48.

Kirzner, I. (1973), *Competition and Entrepreneurship*, Chicago: University of Chicago Press.

Knight, F. [1921 (1971)], *Risk, Uncertainty and Profit* (ed. G.J. Stigler), Chicago: University of Chicago Press.

Lancaster, T. (1992), *The Econometric Analysis of Transition Data*, Cambridge: Cambridge University Press.

Lazear, E. (2004), 'Balanced skills and entrepreneurship', *American Economic Review*, **94**(2), 208–11.

Le, A.T. (1999), 'Empirical studies of self-employment', *Journal of Economic Surveys*, **13**(4), 381–416.

Le Roy, S. and L. Singell (1987), 'Knight on risk and uncertainty', *Journal of Political Economy*, **95**, 394–406.

Leuven, E., H. Oosterbeek and B. van der Klaauw (2003), 'The effect of financial rewards on students' achievement: evidence from a randomized experiment', Tinbergen Institute Discussion Paper 38/03, The Netherlands.

Lindeboom, M. and J. Theeuwes (1991), 'Job duration in the Netherlands: the coexistence of high turnover and permanent job attachment', *Oxford Bulletin of Economics and Statistics*, **53**, 243–64.

Lindh, T. and H. Ohlsson (1996), 'Self-employment and windfall gains: evidence from the Swedish lottery', *Economic Journal*, **106**, 1515–26.

Lucas, R. (1978), 'On the size distribution of business firms', *Bell Journal of Economics*, **9**(2), 508–23.

Maddala, G. (1983), *Limited-dependent and qualitative variables in econometrics*, Cambridge: Cambridge University Press.

Magnac, T. and J. Robin (1994), 'An econometric analysis of labour market transitions using discrete and tenure data', *Labour Economics*, **1**, 327–46.

Marshall, A. [1890 (1930)], *Principles of Economics*, London: Macmillan.

Meager, N. (1992), 'Does unemployment lead to self-employment?', *Small Business Economics*, **4**, 87–103.

Miller, R. (1984), 'Job matching and occupational choice', *Journal of Political Economy*, **92**, 1086–120.

Mincer, J. (1974), *Schooling, Experience and Earnings*, New York: Columbia University Press.

Mood, A., F. Graybill and D. Boes (1986), *Introduction to the Theory of Statistics*, New York and London: McGraw-Hill, international student (third) edition.

Nijman, T. and M. Verbeek (1992), 'Non response in panel data: the impact on estimates of a life cycle consumption function', *Journal of Applied Econometrics*, **7**(3), 243–57.

Parker, S. (2004), *The Economics of Self-employment and Entrepreneurship*, Cambridge: Cambridge University Press.

Parker, S. and C.M. van Praag (2004), 'Schooling, capital constraints and entrepreneurial performance: the endogenous triangle', Tinbergen Institute Discussion Paper 04-106/3, The Netherlands.

Pennings, L., L. Lee and A. van Witteloostuijn (1998), 'Human capital, social capital, and firm dissolution', *Academy of Management Journal*, **41**(4), 425–40.

Peteraf, M. and M. Shanley (1997), 'Getting to know you: a theory of strategic group identity', *Strategic Management Journal*, **18**, 165–86.

Pickles, A. and P.O. Farrell (1987), 'An analysis of entrepreneurial behaviour from male work histories', *Regional Studies*, **21**(5), 425–44.

Poirier, D. (1980), 'Partial observability in bivariate probit models', *Journal of Econometrics*, **12**, 209–17.

Pratt, J. (1964), 'Risk aversion in the small and in the large', *Econometrica*, **32**, 122–36.

Reuber, A. and E. Fischer (1999), 'Understanding the consequences of founders' experience', *Journal of Small Business Management*, **37**(2), 30–45.

Ridder, G. (1987), 'Life cycle patterns in labor market experience, a statistical analysis of labor market histories of adult men', PhD thesis, University of Amsterdam.

Riley, J. (2002), 'Weak and strong signals', *Scandinavian Journal of Economics*, **104**, 213–36.

Robinson, P. and E. Sexton (1994), 'The effect of education and experience on self-employment success', *Journal of Business Venturing*, **9**, 141–56.

Rotter, J. (1966), 'Generalized expectancies for internal versus external control of reinforcement', in *Psychological Monographs: General and Applied*, **80**(1), 1–28.

Rouse, C. (1999), 'Further estimates of the economic return to schooling from a new sample of twins', *Economics of Education Review*, **18**(2), 149–57.

Say, J. [1803 (1971)], *A Treatise on Political Economy or the Production, Distribution and Consumption of Wealth*, New York: A.M. Kelley.

Scherr, F., T. Sugrue and J. Ward (1993), 'Financing the small firm start-up: determinants of debt use', *Journal of Small Business Finance*, **3**(1), 17–36.

Schumpeter, J. [1911 (1934)], *The Theory of Economic Development*, Cambridge, MA: Harvard University Press.

Schumpeter, J. (1939), *Business Cycles*, New York and London: McGraw-Hill.

Shapero, A. (1975), 'The displaced, uncomfortable entrepreneur', *Psychology Today*, **9**, 83–8.

Silva, O. (2004), 'Entrepreneurship: can the jack-of-all-trades attitude be acquired?', CEP Discussion Paper 665.

Spence, A. (1973), *Market Signaling: Information Transfer in Hiring and Related Processes*, Cambridge, MA: Harvard University Press.

Stanworth, J., S. Blythe, B. Granger and C. Stanworth (1989), 'Who becomes an entrepreneur?', *International Small Business Journal*, **8**(1), 11–22.

Storey, D. (1991), 'The birth of new firms. Does unemployment matter?', *Small Business Economics*, **3**, 167–78.

Storey, D. (1994), *Understanding the Small Business Sector*, London and New York: Routledge.

Taylor, M. (1999), 'Survival of the fittest? An analysis of self-employment duration in Britain', *Economic Journal*, **109**, 140–55.

Tucker, I. (1985), 'Use of the decomposition technique to test the educational screening hypothesis', *Economics of Education Review*, **4**(4), 321–6.

Tucker, I. (1987), 'The impact of consumer credentialism on employee and entrepreneur returns to higher education', *Economics of Education Review*, **6**(1), 35–40.

Van der Sluis, J. and C.M. van Praag (2004), 'Economic returns to education for enterpreneurs: the development of a neglected child in the family of economics of education?', *Swedish Economic Policy Review*, **11**(2), 183–226.

Van der Sluis, J., C.M. van Praag and W. Vijverberg (2003), 'Entrepreneurship selection and performance: a meta-analysis of the impact of education in industrialized countries', Tinbergen Institute Discussion Paper 04-046/3, The Netherlands.

Van der Sluis, J., C.M. van Praag and W. Vijverberg (2006), 'Entrepreneurship selection and performance: a meta-analysis of the impact of education in less developed countries', forthcoming in the *World Bank Economic Review*.

Van der Sluis, J., C.M. van Praag and A. van Witteloostuijn (2004), 'The returns to education: a comparative study between entrepreneurs and employees', Tinbergen Institute Discussion Paper 04-104/3, The Netherlands.

Van Praag, C.M. (1996), *Determinants of Successful Entrepreneurship*, Amsterdam: Thesis Publishers.

Van Praag, C.M. (1999), 'Some classic views on entrepreneurship', *De Economist*, **147**(3), 311–35.

Van Praag, C.M. (2003), 'Business survival and success of young small business owners: an empirical analysis', *Small Business Economics*, **21**(1), 1–17.

Van Praag, C.M., N. Bosma and G. de Wit (2003), 'Initial capital constraints hinder entrepreneurial venture performance: an empirical analysis', Tinbergen Institute Discussion Paper 04-047/3, The Netherlands.

Van Praag, C.M. and J. Cramer (2001), 'The roots of entrepreneurship and labour demand: individual ability and low risk aversion', *Economica*, **269**, 45–62.

Van Praag, C.M. and J. van Ophem (1995), 'Determinants of willingness and opportunity to start as an entrepreneur', *Kyklos*, **48**, 513–40.

Wagner, J. (2002), 'Testing Lazear's jack-of-all-trades view of entrepreneurship with German data', IZA Discussion Paper 592.

Weick, K. (1996), 'Drop your tools: an allegory for organizational studies', *Administrative Science Quarterly*, **41**, 301–14.

Wolpin, K. (1977), 'Education and screening', *American Economic Review*, **67**, 949–58.

Wright, M. and P. Westhead (1998), 'Habitual entrepreneurs and angel investors', *Entrepreneurship Theory and Practice*, **22**(4), 5–21.

Index